SPECTACULAR HOMES

of California

AN EXCLUSIVE SHOWCASE OF CALIFORNIA'S FINEST DESIGNERS

Published by

PANACHE
PARTNERS LLC

13747 Montfort Drive, Suite 100
Dallas, Texas 75240
972-661-9884
972-661-2743
www.panache.com

Publishers: Brian G. Carabet and John A. Shand
Editor: Allison Hatfield
Graphic Designer: Emily Kattan

Printed in Malaysia

Distributed by Gibbs Smith, Publisher
800-748-5439

PUBLISHER'S DATA

Spectacular Homes of California

Library of Congress Control Number: 2004117271

ISBN 13: 978-1-933415-13-0
ISBN 10: 1-933415-13-4

First Printing 2006

10 9 8 7 6 5 4 3 2 1

Previous Page: Jerry Hettinger, J. Hettinger Interiors
See page 157 Photograph by Douglas Johnson

This Page: Cheryl Gardner, Cheryl Gardner Interior Design
See page 57 Photograph by Michael Kalla Photography

SPECTACULAR HOMES
of California

AN EXCLUSIVE SHOWCASE OF CALIFORNIA'S FINEST DESIGNERS

INTRODUCTION

was giddy like Christmas morning the day that I met the room of my dreams.

For the inaugural issue of a new shelter magazine I'd happily accepted the assignment to become a "client" of a talented interior designer. His job was to take me step by step through the design process, sorting through my confusion and creating for me a space that uniquely reflected my tastes. My job was to write about the experience. Though the "budget" was unlimited and my "living room" was a set in a photographer's studio, everything else remained true to my lifestyle.

When I consulted with my designer we talked about my needs and I gave him tear sheets of objects and furniture whose shapes or colors thrilled me. Within a few days, he'd drawn up a floor plan, and then we went shopping. The results of our conversations and trips to furniture showrooms nearly brought me to tears: he delivered a room that was an impeccable interpretation of my truest self, of everything I am and all I ever hope to become.

And, I dare say, that is the sincerest goal of every one of the 56 interior designers featured in Spectacular Homes of California.

In glorious four-color photography, this volume showcases the work of esteemed, award-winning designers recognized for their talents in the Golden State and beyond. Some, like the affable Tommy Chambers or the unpretentious Paul Wiseman, are brilliant and established industry leaders who through their long and illustrious careers have had tremendous impact on the interior design community worldwide. Others, like Valerie Pugliese, have only begun to make their marks but show the promise of success.

Regardless of experience, whether they've been designing for two years or 32, all of the professionals in this book have a few things in common. Without exception, they are passionate about great design, whether ultra contemporary or wholly traditional. They eschew trends and strive for classic appeal with personal imprint. They have learned to set their own egos aside and really listen to their clients. And, of course, they have exquisite style and an innate ability to turn a homeowner's wish list into reality.

Unlike the dazzling spaces featured within, my dream room wasn't real. I didn't get to keep so much as the orchid that had been carefully placed on the tea table, never mind the $25,000 Peter Zimmerman painting. But it inspires me to this day. I hope Spectacular Homes does the same for you.

Cheers,

Allison Hatfield

Allison Hatfield
Editor

TABLE OF CONTENTS

DESIGNER: **Tommy Chambers**, Tommy Chambers Interiors, Inc., *Page 33*

LOS ANGELES

AN EXCLUSIVE SHOWCASE OF LOS ANGELES' FINEST DESIGNERS

carolinebaker

CAROLINE BAKER INTERIOR DESIGN

LEFT
Art adds to the color and drama of the Grand Entry Rotunda in the 2001 Pasadena Showcase House of Design featuring Scalamandré fabrics.
Photograph by Cameron Carothers

RIGHT
Color accents the combination of modern and craftsman in this contemporary Beverly Hills living room.
Photograph by Cameron Carothers

Imagine...walking into a home filled with breathtaking, glorious, elegant colors, and you will experience what Caroline Baker wholeheartedly believes is the essence of great interior design. An energetic, fun-loving woman herself, Caroline places color at the forefront of all her designs. "Color drives emotion," Caroline explains. "It brings life to a room, and it is totally necessary for a space to be comfortable." Her style is elegant yet livable, warm and inviting with a harmonious blend of colors. Caroline is happiest when her clients are surrounded by the colors they love.

Great design does not exist in one mind alone, according to Caroline. For this reason, she goes to great lengths to understand her clients' ideas and needs, asking questions and carefully considering the answers. This process allows for the alignment of perspectives, ultimately leading to thoughtful and beautiful interiors.

Steering clear of a cookie-cutter look, Caroline has earned a reputation for tasteful environments that are highly customized for her clients. "An elegant use of colors and textures results from actively listening to and collaborating with my clients to make the perfect home for them," she says. As an avid collector of art from around the world, Caroline understands the importance of incorporating the cherished items her clients love — from African sculptures to English china — into their homes. And though she guides her clients toward lovely and engaging design solutions, she never imposes an absolute edict on anyone.

"In addition to color, wonderful art is an essential part of great design. But even more important is knowing when to stop," she says. Over-designing is as much a design faux pas as under-designing, something Caroline's clients don't have to worry about. She never stops short of stunning! "When my clients walk into their newly designed homes and say 'Wow,' I feel like I've done a fantastic job."

ABOVE LEFT
Clean lines and soothing color create a sense of sanctuary for this Beverly Hills bedroom.
Photograph by Cameron Carothers

ABOVE RIGHT
Sweeping curves and warm colors create a dramatic yet inviting kitchen in Claremont (a collaboration with Hartman Baldwin Design/Build).
Photograph by Cameron Carothers

FACING PAGE
Vibrant colors enliven this traditional living room in La Canada featuring Scalamandré fabrics.
Photograph by Cameron Carothers

Q&A
more about caroline

WHAT PERSONAL INDULGENCE DOES SHE SPEND THE MOST MONEY ON?

Unable to choose between clothes and food, Caroline says her greatest personal luxuries are evening gowns by former Halston creative director and fellow FIDM graduate Kevan Hall, and dinners at Bistro 45, a well-known Pasadena restaurant.

WHAT IS THE HIGHEST COMPLIMENT CAROLINE HAS BEEN PAID PROFESSIONALLY?

Caroline has been asked to participate in the Pasadena Showcase House of Design for many years and her designs have been featured on the covers of the U section of the *Pasadena Star News* and the Design section of the *L.A. Times*, as well as on NBC and Channel 9.

WHY DOES CAROLINE LOVE DOING BUSINESS IN CALIFORNIA?

Her creativity is inspired by the vast array of architectural styles prevalent in the state. From traditional Mediterranean homes by Garrett Van Pelt and Sylvanus Marston in Pasadena to modern and contemporary homes in Beverly Hills and Claremont to traditional homes in Manhattan Beach and La Canada, the types of projects Caroline takes on are as individual as their owners. In tackling such diverse jobs, Caroline says, "I try to be sensitive to the environment created by the architecture of the home and create a design that allows the home to reach its full potential."

Caroline Baker Interior Design
Caroline Baker, Allied Member, ASID
745 South Marengo Ave.
Pasadena, CA 91106
626.796.6670
Fax: 626.796.4064
www.carolinebakerdesign.com

kathleen**beall**

BEALL DESIGN GROUP, INC.

Excellent design is in the details," says Kathleen Beall, ASID, CID, president and principal interior designer at Beall Design Group, Inc. Attention to detail is the signature trademark of this unique firm, which approaches design from an architectural and interior perspective.

Kathleen's U.C. Davis education — she earned a degree in environmental design — helped shape her design approach. Her style is to look at the entire project, even if she is to undertake just a part of the project, to ensure balance and flow. This sensitivity to the blending of design aspects has given her work a reputation as being warm and inviting. Clients often say the spaces that Kathleen creates for them are so comfortable they never want to leave.

With more than 20 years' experience, Beall Design Group has also earned a reputation that inspires faith and trust from high-end clients who demand excellence. Available for as little or as much as a job requires, the firm shines when given free reign. In fact, many of their projects are second homes located far from their owners, who might never even see their new residences until they walk in with their clothes, Kathleen says. Her company provides turnkey services, from pre-construction to the finishing touches, playing an invaluable role as the eyes, ears, and voice for their conscientious clientele.

"We are fortunate," Kathleen says, "to have clients who enable us to do our very best work." And that work has not gone unrecognized: One kitchen remodel earned the firm prestigious recognition when it was chosen from among those in 11 Western United States and Western Canada by the Pacific Coast Builders Conference to receive the Gold Nugget Award of Merit.

ABOVE
Embraced the client's personal collection of the Asian arts. Private residence, living room, Rancho Mirage, CA.
Photograph by Barbara White

RIGHT
Custom-designed dining table features a suspended Balinese mask looking up at the table quests. Private residence, dining room and kitchen, Rancho Mirage, CA.
Photograph by Barbara White

FACING PAGE LEFT
Custom onyx and limestone are the natural materials featured. Private residence, master bedroom, Dana Point, CA.
Photograph by Barbara White

FACING PAGE RIGHT
Private residence, entry, dining room, and living room, Dana Point, CA.
Photograph by Barbara White

Q&A

more about kathleen

WHAT ONE ELEMENT OF STYLE OR PHILOSOPHY HAS SHE STUCK WITH FOR YEARS THAT STILL WORKS FOR YOU TODAY?

Quality. I always tell people that it is better to have one fabulous piece than to buy many pieces of a lesser quality or that are less interesting.

WHAT IS THE MOST UNUSUAL/EXPENSIVE/DIFFICULT DESIGN OR TECHNIQUE KATHLEEN HAS USED IN ONE OF HER PROJECTS?

Years ago, Kathleen was part of a design team that created a fireplace for a desert home that incorporated a fossilized palm frond 10 feet high and 10 feet wide. "It was incredible," she says.

Beall Design Group, Inc.
Kathleen Beall, ASID, CID
P.O. Box 1852
Redland, CA 92373
909.335.4887
www.bealldesigngroup.com

jennifer**bevan-montoya**

JENNIFER BEVAN INTERIORS

Jennifer Bevan-Montoya might have been an architect but she didn't want to do the math. Instead, she married an architecture school graduate and became an interior designer. It was hardly a compromise when you consider Jennifer's success in the last 25 years.

The Los Angeles native graduated magna cum laude from Woodbury University, but her design career began even before she finished school, when she landed a job at an interior design firm. But her interest in bettering people's homes began even earlier. "When I was a child, I would ride in the car with my parents. I would see houses and think of ways to make them more attractive," she remembers. Improving home environments is something Jennifer became very good at.

As one of the area's leading interior designers, she was among just 20 L. A. designers chosen to work with Richard Landry on the Esquire Magazine House in 2004. She's a 10th time participant in the Pasadena Showcase House, and her work has been featured numerous times on HGTV and in regional publications. Professional accolades notwithstanding, Jennifer's most prized compliments come from repeat clients and other interior designers who ask her to work on their homes.

Drawing inspiration from her travels, fashion, and a dedicated team of six employees, Jennifer blends classic with contemporary to offer her clients unique and inspired choices for transforming their rooms into distinctive living spaces. "I believe design is more than just an artistic arrangement of

LEFT
The existing ceiling is graced by an original 1927 mahogany coffered ceiling. A magnificent palace-size antique "Sarouk" area rug grounds the room bringing it together. Custom-carved arched cornice holds silk damask drapery while antique fautliz chairs direct attention to the center of the room. Houlès trim on sofa. Wallace Neff architecture; Mediterranean style.
Photograph by Peter Christiansen Valli

furnishings," she says. "A truly beautiful room creates a sensation that is as energetic as it is harmonious."

To that end, the designer always begins with the client's guidance and with the goal of creatively providing the homeowner with a level of quality and elegance that surpasses anything that person has experienced to that point. And within each of her designs there is a hint of Asian influence, which Jennifer says lends peace and balance to any style.

ABOVE LEFT
Fine cherry wood library cabinets line the wall. Armillary rests on pedestal next to Dennis & Leen soft glove leather chairs. Sumptuous drapery with tasseled over swag frames the window. Painted ceiling on canvas brings Old World design to the room.
Photograph by Michael Wells

ABOVE RIGHT
Minton Spiedel light fixtures, walnut-stained cabinets and cast stone hood over stove enrich this grand kitchen. Gialled renze marble counter tops, antiqued Giallo marble floor and Rosa Verona honed marble island top add engaging, natural elements.
Photograph by Peter Christiansen Valli

FACING PAGE
Reclaimed exterior space returned to original Loggia assisted by hand-painted ceiling and reclaimed pavers from provincial France.
Photograph by Peter Christiansen Valli

Q&A

more about jennifer

WHAT PERSONAL INDULGENCE DOES JENNIFER SPEND THE MOST MONEY ON?

That's easy, she says. Shoes.

WHAT COLOR BEST DESCRIBES HER AND WHY?

Jennifer is fond of all colors. Her preference depends on her mood and the job she's working on. "Perhaps I am a bit of a chameleon," she says, "because my favorites are always changing." Currently, the designer leans toward orange, which she feels is "hot and sassy."

WHAT BOOK IS SHE READING RIGHT NOW?

Jennifer is reading *Harry Potter* with her 11-year-old son, Kent.

HOW CAN YOU TELL SHE LIVES IN SOUTHERN CALIFORNIA?

Like most people in the area, she's always in her car and her cell phone has become a permanent appendage.

WHAT IS THE BEST PART ABOUT BEING AN INTERIOR DESIGNER?

When we place the final accessory and the rooms look great. The pleasure of knowing that our clients are happy and comfortable in their beautiful home.

Jennifer Bevan Interiors
Jennifer Bevan-Montoya, ASID, CID
729 Mission Street, Suite 400
South Pasadena, CA 91030
626.799.9924

julia**brill**

MASION CHIC, INC.

For the last 15 years, first under the name Ventana Design and now as Maison Chic, Julia Brill has been making her mark on the L.A. design world. Were it not for her mother, Julia might have chosen a different career. As a child, the designer spent long hours watching the prominent L.A. artist, work. And it was her mother who introduced Julia to interior design and inspired her to pursue her passion for art and love of architecture.

After attending the University of Southern California, where she earned her undergraduate degree in communications, Julia received a degree in interior design at UCLA while interning with a cousin, a prominent (now-retired) designer in the area. With all of her clients, Julia plays a dual role: talented interior designer and patient advisor, steering clients toward choices that make sense for the architectural elements of their homes to complement their lifestyles. Communicating with clients is an all-important aspect of every project, and she often serves as a liaison between technical crews and other interior designers.

Julia prides herself in creating continuity throughout a home and remaining true to the style of the structure. In fact, maintaining architectural integrity is something she insists upon. Using her knowledge and understanding of architectural space, Julia customizes each design, focusing on clean lines, subtle colors, and modern sensibilities and combines them with earthy materials and international accents. Quietly persistent and committed to an outcome that satisfies both form and

function, Julia listens to her clients carefully and guides them through examples they can relate to. In that way, she is able to provide homeowners design that suits both their personal tastes as well as the interior space available.

Something new she's giving homeowners is a cutting-edge solution to incorporating technology into interior design. She recently launched a line of fine art frames with an integrated speaker system that makes the presence of a flat-screen TV in a room more appealing. This collection can be seen in her virtual home showroom at the Pacific Design Center.

In her free time, Julia is a doting mom, a voracious reader, and a woman who's traveled to nearly 20 countries. Casual yet cultured, the 37-year-old Golden State native loves living in Southern California because of the many and varied social opportunities: She might see the King Tut exhibit at Los Angeles County Museum of Art in the morning and take in a David Byrne concert with her 85-year-old mother-in-law at the Bowl at night.

FACING PAGE
Marble floors and Calcutta gold marble countertops combined with an etched limestone backsplash liner offers a relaxed sophistication to this gourmet cook's kitchen. To provide the perfect ambience to this timeless architecture, the room is sun kissed by natural lighting from a skylight and accented by English antiques — all hand selected from over 60 shops by interior designer Brill and interior decorator Milena Koncar.

RIGHT
Free-hand classic: Recessed medicine cabinets that double as mirrors with concealed outlets for his and hers electronic toothbrushes hang delicately above a marble-top breakfront. Subtle accents provide warmth and comfort to this modest space.

Q&A more about julia

WHAT COLOR BEST DESCRIBES HER?

Chocolate. Because, like Julia's designs, it has natural beauty and stimulates the senses.

WHICH L.A. HOME IMPRESSES JULIA THE MOST?

Julia grew up in a house built in the 1920s and she finds that period magnificently inspiring. The former Harold Lloyd estate — a beautiful and significant example of Mediterranean/Italian Renaissance style, built in 1928 — is her favorite home in the area.

WHAT DESIGN/ARCHITECTURAL/BUILDING TECHNIQUES WOULD SHE LIKE TO ELIMINATE?

With a penchant for all things Old World, Julia finds track homes and strip malls monotonous and lacking in character.

Maison Chic, Inc.
Julia Brill, Allied Member, ASID
Pacific Design Center
8687 Melrose Avenue, Suite M04
West Hollywood, CA 90069
818.783.6789
www.maisonchic.com

barclaybutera

BARCLAY BUTERA, INC.

R obert Frost wrote: "Two roads diverged in a yellow wood/I took the one less traveled by./And that has made all the difference."

Like the famed poet, interior designer Barclay Butera has always felt that he chose to break convention — and that decision set the tone for his life's work.

Though he attended Brigham Young University, earning a degree in political science and economics, and thought about becoming an attorney, Barclay returned to his true passion — design — within one year of embarking on law school. That was when, at age 25, he took the opportunity to create and run his own stylish case goods company in Los Angeles.

The California native's interest in interior design was not unfounded: His career path was, undoubtedly, influenced by his mother, who designed the interiors of private clients' homes worldwide. Barclay worked side by side with her every summer as a boy, traveling the country and gaining a perspective on the industry from a young age. It is to his parents and especially to his maternal grandfather — who worked for 30 years as a traveling salesman for General Mills — that Barclay credits his unrelenting work ethic, which has propelled him to the top of his craft and drives him to create for his clients sophisticated, elegant, and livable environments — "Their own personal havens," he says.

LEFT
Barclay Butera gave a Southwestern-style Palm Springs retreat a well-traveled feel with a Mexican chandelier featuring antique-mirrored glass; a Buddha, among other Asian elements; and a refreshing blue-and-white, ocean-inspired palette. The Hampton Sofa is from the Barclay Butera Home line.
Photo courtesy of Barclay Butera Inc.;
Photograph by Mark Lohman.

Barclay's style is transitional, and it begins by combining the look of the late British Colonial Empire with European, Far East, and American traditional influences, and by blending furniture and pattern-on-pattern fabrics in warm colors. He then adds a twist. Though he takes cues from the past, Barclay breaks established convention and prefers to explore the limits of design and learn as he goes. To wit: early in his career, the designer surpassed that era's trend of matched furniture sets and moved to an approach that mixes old with new. By drawing inspiration from a client's heritage, then incorporating his own vision — which often includes elements from the Gatsby to the Rat Pack eras — Barclay creates interiors that are at once meaningful and fresh.

With every project, Barclay focuses on listening to the clients and giving them what they want. "I'm a huge believer in 'a client for life,'" he says. "I instill this in my employees. It's always about the customer, the quality, and service."

FACING PAGE
Tonal blues and white — accenting oceanfront living — are mixed with wicker, mahogany, and a cozy bench to create a comfortable breakfast nook in a Newport Beach home.
Photo courtesy of Barclay Butera Inc.;
Photograph by Bob Hodson

TOP RIGHT
Barclay combined earthy tones and materials — a Persian rug, red accents against leather, woven chairs — in this Palm Springs home. The Doheny Sofa is from the Barclay Butera Home line.
Photo courtesy of Barclay Butera Inc.;
Photograph by Mark Lohman

BOTTOM RIGHT
Eclecticism is very much Barclay's style, as is seen in this Laguna Beach home that includes a contemporary coffee table; Barclay's Somerset sofa, which has a classic English arm; blue and white jars influenced by Colonial Britain; trophy antlers; and raffia wallpaper.
Photo courtesy of Barclay Butera Inc.

ABOVE
The blue hues on this dramatic and luxurious Palm Springs patio harmonize with those used inside the house.
Photo courtesy of Barclay Butera Inc.;
Photograph by Mark Lohman.

FACING PAGE
Black, camel, and white with touch of red give the master bedroom a Rat Pack feel in Desi Arnaz Jr.'s former home, a mid-century modern overlooking Los Angeles. Lucille Ball purchased the bronze light fixtures that still hang in the room; they contrast nicely with the Getty Photo images on Lucite.
Photo courtesy of Barclay Butera Inc.

It is within that framework that Barclay strives to redefine luxury, much like his professional idol, Ralph Lauren, whom Barclay admires for his consistent efforts in creating a beautiful, timeless, and attainable lifestyle.

Barclay's 12-year-old company comprises a national corporation featuring more than 100 employees, five exquisite retail collection showrooms that showcase the Barclay Butera Home brand (including his signature furniture — available at more than 300 retailers nationally — and soon expanding to textiles, lamps, accessories, and home fragrance) as well as several other top U.S. design lines, and a manufacturing plant in Los Angeles.

Q&A
more about barclay

WHAT DESIGN PHILOSOPHY HAS HE STUCK WITH THROUGH THE YEARS THAT STILL SERVES HIM TODAY?

The cornerstones of Barclay's business are "integrity, consistency, and my core beliefs, which include a very strong work ethic and being a man of my word," he says. Barclay embraces the Rat Pack/Auntie Mame era, when homes' interiors were designed to draw people into conversation. Visually, he enjoys bold, unexpected color schemes and draws inspiration from fashion's Bill Blass, Paul Smith, Trina Turk, and Tory Burch.

AWARDS AND RECOGNITION?

Barclay is nationally recognized for elegant yet progressive design in upholstery and case goods. He has been featured in many national publications including *House Beautiful* (Top 125 Designers), *Elements of Living* (Top 50 Designers), the *Wall Street Journal*, *InStyle*, *InTouch*, *Western Interiors & Design*, *Country Home*, *Coastal Living*, *Elle Decor*, and *The Los Angeles Times*. He has appeared on *Extra!*, *Find!*, *Beautiful Homes & Great Estates*, and various home improvement shows.

Barclay Butera Home Showrooms:

Los Angeles, CA/Pacific Design Center
310.289.2885

Newport Beach, CA
949.650.1730

New York/D&D Building
212.207.8665

Barclay Butera Collection Showrooms:

Los Angeles, CA
323.634.0200

Newport Beach, CA
949.650.8570

Park City, UT
435.649.5540

Barclay Butera, Inc.
Barclay Butera, ASID
www.barclaybutera.com
www.barclaybuterahome.com

tommychambers

TOMMY CHAMBERS INTERIORS, INC.

LEFT
A mahogany and glass front door opens into a Laguna Beach entry with stained concrete floor and a colorful custom raku ceramic installation.
Photograph by David Phelps

RIGHT
This entry also boasts a custom Chambers' designed "sunburst" rug manufactured by Hokanson, Inc. and a passage to the guest suite.
Photograph by David Phelps

"His level of commitment, professionalism, enthusiasm, and quality of work is unsurpassed." "His trained eye and natural talents create the most pleasing and accommodating of spaces." "[Tommy has] shown us how beautiful things can look again." Such are the comments of Tommy Chambers's clients. The last he considers to be the highest compliment any client has paid him. Tommy, a renowned industry leader, believes that his fundamental responsibility as a designer is to his clients. He seeks to create spaces that express clients' individual personalities and interests — to express their ideas of what's welcoming and comfortable. Though he occasionally does carte blanche work, the 37-year-old designer prefers to collaborate with homeowners. "There's a real reward in getting inside someone's head and discovering what that person wants from a room, then giving that to them in a way that is timeless and livable," he says. "That's usually more satisfying for them and for me."

A man of great character and charisma, described by a colleague as "disarming in his authenticity, compassion, and warmth," Tommy grew up in a tight-knit family in rural west Texas. He earned a degree in architecture from Texas A&M in 1990, then moved to Los Angeles. After a five-year apprenticeship with Joan Axelrod Interiors, he founded the award-winning firm of Chambers & Murray with partner Bill Murray, where he spent eight years as head of the interiors department

and senior business operations manager. Four years ago, Tommy set out on his own; and his eponymous company has quickly developed a reputation for fresh, updated, traditional and contemporary interior design executed with wit and charm.

By design, Chambers has no signature style. He spends a great deal of time getting to know his clients and says personal impressions often determine the elements of his rooms. This working method creates subtle, thoughtful, and polished interiors — and, quite often, close and enduring relationships with clients. Personally involved in every project his small firm takes on, Tommy listens to clients carefully, taking comprehensive account of their wants and needs,

TOP LEFT
The dining room window walls disappear for unobstructed views of the Pacific while dining on solid walnut chairs and an oak dining table.
Photograph by David Phelps

BOTTOM LEFT
The kitchen has solid oak wood floors, Carrera marble counter tops and limestone island top with custom stainless steel cabinetry.
Photograph by David Phelps

FACING PAGE
The dining room steps down into the living room with its Paul Smith "swirl" wool rug, vintage "Dunbar" coffee table and upholstery by Tommy Chambers and Michael Berman.
Photograph by David Phelps

as well as their budgets. In that way he is able to give a Manhattan resident a calming, meditative Park Avenue escape from the bustling city; or restore an authentic 1920s feel to a Los Feliz home; or provide a Laguna Beach couple with a boldly modern yet comfortable space in which to enjoy an expansive view of the Pacific.

And regardless of the location or look, all of Tommy's interiors have one thing in common: They are organic, reflecting the mood of familiarity in which they were conceived, and conveying a quiet, confident sense of personal history.

FACING PAGE
A crewel and silk fabric grace an entry table on black and white marble floors of a fully restored Wallace Neff house in Pasadena.
Photograph by David Phelps

RIGHT
A Newport Beach reading room decorated with Brunschwig & Fils fabric, antique table, custom-designed etergere and an Indian elephant table found at a flea market.
Photograph by David Phelps

more about tommy

WHAT DOES TOMMY ENJOY MOST ABOUT BEING AN INTERIOR DESIGNER?

"Making something out of nothing," he says.

WHAT IS THE MOST IMPRESSIVE PROJECT HE'S BEEN INVOLVED IN TO DATE?

Though he's worked on the homes of pop music icon Justin Timberlake, actors Courtney Cox and David Arquette, filmmaker John Hughes, Norman Lear, and Emmy-winning director/producer Todd Holland, Tommy says that Cindy Costner's La Canada home was for him, his biggest accomplishment. "It totally reflects Cindy and her family in comfortable, warm and pleasant spaces, and yet, every element, head to toe, is original design," he says.

Tommy Chambers Interiors, Inc.
Tommy Chambers, ASID, IIDA
1146 North Gardner Street
Los Angeles, CA 90046
323.436.7565
www.tommychambersinteriors.com

johncole

JOHN COLE INTERIOR DESIGN

When creating an interior, John Cole looks to two things: the architecture of the structure and his client's desires. By tuning in to those driving factors, he renders innovative interiors that are sophisticated and practical, comfortable and fashionable.

Though he began his career training at the Fashion Institute of Design & Merchandising with the intention of becoming a clothing designer, John quickly realized a zeal for interior design. After 26 years, he can honestly say that he's never tired of it. "It's always fresh, always interesting, always different," he says.

A stickler for designing with a project's architecture in mind, John is best known for a style he defines as "European Country." Many of his rooms are in a French Normandy, English, Mediterranean, or Tuscan vein. That's not to say, however, that he avoids contemporary work. In fact, he says, he finds the different sources such jobs require to be an invigorating departure from his norm.

Either way, John is vigilant about creating a continuous, pleasing transition not only from room to room but also inside and out. In fact, his portfolio includes a goodly number of patios, and landscaping is one of his hobbies. He often gets involved with the landscaping on a project, collaborating with the landscape architect to ensure a cohesive flow between a home's interior and exterior.

Describing himself as an old soul, the 46-year-old designer, charming and vivacious, is passionate about antiques. He marvels at objects that can survive the ravages of hundreds of years and cannot remember a time when he didn't gravitate toward beautiful old things. Forced to choose between a fine antique

LEFT
The colorful palette of this living room was extracted from the English chintz with corresponding layers of patterns and textures.
Photograph by Peter Christiansen Valli

armoire and a new car, John says he'd take the armoire every time. And whenever possible he incorporates antiques, fine reproductions, or custom pieces made to look antique into his clients' homes, using them to impart warmth and character in his designs.

Great fabrics also play a large role in John's design work. As with antiques, the designer is naturally drawn to beautiful and important textiles; so much so that he will purchase fabric he feels an immediate affinity for without a predetermined use for it, anticipating a future need or simply fulfilling a desire to populate his own space with color and texture. By the same token, he overbuys for his clients, keeping a stock of their fabrics should pets or kids damage their upholstery.

The latter is just one example of how John fulfills his twin goals of "customer satisfaction as opposed to customer service" and creating interiors that look as good 10 years down the road as they do the day they are completed.

ABOVE LEFT
A large European-styled, exterior fireplace provides a dramatic focal point for a terrace surrounded by the lush greenery of a country estate.
Photograph by Peter Christiansen Valli

ABOVE RIGHT
Custom wicker and iron furnishings fill this classic Tudor gallery, where the architectural surroundings set the stage for a comfortable, yet elegant outdoor living and dining area.
Photograph by Peter Christiansen Valli

FACING PAGE TOP
Architectural display cases featuring a collection of French majolica provide the backdrop for a luxurious dining experience.
Photograph by Peter Christiansen Valli

FACING PAGE BOTTOM
Seamlessly added to an existing estate, the carved stone mantel and custom hand-painted, coffered ceilings set forth the design for this Italianate family room.
Photograph by Peter Christiansen Valli

TOP LEFT
Lavish accoutrements preside over a gracious dining area set in a sumptuous palette of apricots, teals and browns borrowed from the dramatic pattern of the Egyptian, hand-knotted rug.
Photograph by Peter Christiansen Valli

BOTTOM LEFT
Refurbished walnut paneling and original leaded-glass door bookcases are combined with a tone-on-tone striped wall covering and plaster cast crown moldings, providing a timeless backdrop in which to pursue one's literary interests.
Photograph by Peter Christiansen Valli

FACING PAGE
Striking a stylish balance between masculine and feminine, the combinational use of patterns found in the leopard-rose carpet and floral linen upholstery and bedding provide a classic, tranquil retreat.
Photograph by Peter Christiansen Valli

Q&A more about john

WHAT IS ONE THING MOST PEOPLE DON'T KNOW ABOUT JOHN?

He is a prolific and creative cook.

WHAT COLOR BEST DESCRIBES HIM?

John most relates to chocolate brown for its drama and versatility. "It can be integrated into most any room," he says.

YOU WOULDN'T KNOW IT, BUT HIS FRIENDS WOULD TELL YOU THAT...

John is, in his words, a "certified open-house looky-loo."

WHO HAS HAD THE GREATEST IMPACT ON HIS CAREER?

The designer draws inspiration from legendary tastemaker Nancy Lancaster and the dynamic repro duo Stephanie Pineo and René Gregorius. He describes René's home as "understated" and "drop-dead gorgeous" and counts it as the most impressive he's ever visited.

WHAT BOOK IS JOHN READING RIGHT NOW?

He's reading two books, actually, both design-related — *Nancy Lancaster: Her Life, Her World, Her Art,* by Robert Becker, and *Sister: the Life of Legendary Interior Decorator Mrs. Henry Parish II*, by Apple Parish Bartlett and Susan Bartlett Crater.

WHAT DOES HE LIKE MOST ABOUT DOING BUSINESS IN LOS ANGELES?

The beauty and abundance of choices that the area offers.

John Cole Interior Design
John Cole
8866 Collingwood Drive
Los Angeles, CA 90069
310.659.9034

beth**devermont**

DEVERMONT DESIGN GROUP

Born and raised in Los Angeles and designing since childhood, Beth Devermont took on her first career interior design project in 1977 with the remodel of a law office. Since that time, Beth has earned a reputation for interiors that reflect depth and emotion, becoming a respected leader in her field.

Long on creativity and broad in her range of styles, Beth is endlessly artistic and innovative with materials. For example, for one particular condo residence she installed an etched commercial glass door; in another she encased a mirror in limestone to hide an unmovable pipe. She comes to each project with a particular design vision: "I like to think of myself as painting on a six-sided canvas," she says. "My job is to be responsive to my clients and serve as an interpreter of their needs and wishes."

Beth inherited her flair for design from her mother, who also had elegant taste and an eye for distinction. It is certainly from her that the designer intuited how to balance color, scale, and shape. Her mother was most definitely the type of parent who emboldened her child to live — and design — with grace and passion. "Once I start a project," Beth says, "I can't turn it off. It is constantly evolving in my mind, I am continually inspired not only by what's inside of me but also by what's out there," she says, referring to the treasure trove of resources and talented tradesmen in the L.A. area.

In addition to doing kitchens remodels, which are among her favorite projects, Beth is also a wonderful cook. Main dishes are her specialty, and she likes to incorporate unusual spices — something that translates to her designs. Like the meals she prepares, the environments she creates are rich and inviting and full of life.

ABOVE & FACING PAGE
A new spin on "Before and After" — These two rooms were done from the identical original floor plan for two different clients, in two different styles, on two different floors. Remodeling and interior design by designer.
Photograph by Peter Christiansen Valli & Mel Weinstein

RIGHT
Overlooking mountain and sea, this corner terrace grouping of all-weather woven furniture from JANUS et Cie is perfect for relaxation.
Photograph by Michael Kalla

more about beth

WHAT DOES BETH LIKE MOST ABOUT BEING AN INTERIOR DESIGNER?

"The 'high' that I get upon completion of a project," she says. 'I love working with people. I love creating. And I love when it's done and it's beautiful."

WHAT PERSONAL INDULGENCE DOES SHE SPEND THE MOST MONEY ON?

A woman who takes good care of herself, Beth treats herself to regular facials and does yoga at the gym.

WHAT COLOR BEST DESCRIBES HER?

Lavender, a hue that connotes both creativity and gentle strength and is as lovely as the designer herself.

Devermont Design Group
Beth Devermont, ASID, CID
1015 Gayley Avenue, Suite 1264
Los Angeles, CA 90024
310.472.6449

robin**dorman**

ROBIN DORMAN DESIGN CONCEPTS

To date, Robin Dorman's most impressive and challenging project has been her own 11,000-square-foot home. Nestled in a park-like setting on four acres, construction on Stratford Manor began in 1996. The estate sat unfinished until it was purchased by Robin and her husband in 2000. The enormous task of completing the house in three months required 50 to 70 tradesmen a day making quick, confident decisions. Today, the La Canada property is a stunning showcase for and testament to Robin's extraordinary talents.

A respected leader in her field, Robin opened Robin Dorman Design Concepts 16 years ago. She does a great deal of kitchen and bath design, as well as a high volume of complete home and office interiors. Robin often works on her clients' homes from the beginning stages, with the belief that if the hardscape looks good and functions well, the soft goods will follow.

Her office includes a 500-square-foot resource center packed with one-of-a-kind and unusual textiles and embellishments. One of her three staff designers acts as a librarian for the center, keeping the stock organized and continually replenished. The fabrics naturally lead to dramatic window treatments, which are a company specialty and a customer demand. "Fabrics don't have to be fancy," Robin says, "but gorgeous textiles make a room feel warm and cozy. Luscious textures make you feel good about a space."

The personal attention clients get from Robin and her staff also pleases clients. Though she does 40 to 50 projects a year, Robin finds time to focus on each job as if it were her only one. "We are very hands-on and accessible," she says. And her clients can rest assured that the outcome of their designer's efforts will be a comfortable and timeless interior customized to their hopes and dreams.

Q&A

more about robin

WHAT PERSONAL INDULGENCE DOES ROBIN SPEND THE MOST MONEY ON?

A former buyer for Burdines and Saks Fifth Avenue, she loves shoes and accessories. "They go hand in hand and finish an outfit like the final touches of a room," she says.

WHAT COLOR BEST DESCRIBES HER?

Robin says she most relates to pink for its happy, feminine connotations, and she shares those qualities.

WHAT ONE THING DO MOST PEOPLE NOT KNOW ABOUT ROBIN?

An accomplished musician, she sang and played 13 instruments in college. In addition to voice, her concentrations were piano and guitar.

WHAT IS THE BEST PART OF BEING AN INTERIOR DESIGNER?

"My personal relationships with my clients, who often become good friends," she says. "I love being part of creating the environments they enjoy coming home to."

IF YOU COULD ELIMINATE ONE DESIGN/ ARCHITECTURAL/BUILDING TECHNIQUE OR STYLE FROM THE WORLD, WHAT WOULD IT BE?

Acoustic cottage cheese ceilings. I hate them.

Robin Dorman Design Concepts
Robin Dorman, ASID
4033 Chevy Chase Drive
La Canada, CA 91011
818.952.0103

ABOVE
Custom cabinetry with porcelain crackle finish are featured in this open gourmet kitchen. High coffered ceiling and dramatic wall coloring add panache.
Photograph by Peter Christiansen Valli

FACING PAGE TOP
This indoor/outdoor media room is the perfect entertainer's retreat. It accommodates dining, hanging out in the spa or just movie watching.
Photograph by Peter Christiansen Valli

FACING PAGE BOTTOM
Beautiful mahogany paneling sets off this exquisite library. Partners' desk from Baker, Knapp & Tubbs.
Photograph by Weldon Brewster

suzannefurst

SUZANNE FURST INTERIORS

It's funny how we all find our avenues," says Suzanne Furst, who found her calling as an interior designer while remodeling her own home. Today, the New York City native specializes in residential design from concept to completion. All of her projects provide a sense of warmth, serenity, and balance while strictly adhering to the adage that form follows function.

Working in all styles (Old World, Zen contemporary, Retro-Modern, Far Eastern, Shabby Chic — "You name it, I've done it," she says), Suzanne weaves a common thread through all of her interiors: comfort and a sense of well-being and continuity within and between spaces. She loves her work and above all else, thrives in the face of a design challenge.

Extremely detail-oriented and with the objective of meeting clients' specific tastes, much of her work is custom, from cabinetry to furniture and upholstered pieces to draperies and bedding. For example, for her own home, responding to the need for more light in her living room, she designed etched-glass murals permanently set into a curved wall and lit on both sides with fiber optics. The continuing landscape is a practical work of art.

ABOVE & RIGHT
HGTV's Designer Challenge Kitchen and Dining Room: The challenge of this space was to create two functional rooms out of four non functional ones. Kitchen storage was maximized by custom cabinetry details. Non-supportive decorative beams, warm wood floors and sleek cabinetry create a trendy shabby chic motif. The dining room contains an added bonus of a family play area connected to the kitchen through a peninsula bar and wine storage area. The window seat conceals a children's toy storage.
Photographs by Henry Cabala Photography

FACING PAGE
Meditation Retreat: This fully ecological space proves that stylized design can be achieved through the use of sustainable, non-toxic products, recycled woods and natural fibers.
Photograph by Tim Street-Porter

Throughout her 20-year career, Suzanne has balanced her professional life with community service. Her pro bono work for various healthcare facilities, including USC Children's Hospital and the Ronald McDonald House in Hollywood, has been a calming force for those in need of medical assistance. Most recently the former president of the L. A. Chapter of ASID spearheaded the Design Showcase at Greystone Mansion, which was fueled by her desire to help restore a landmark estate and educate the general public on the important contributions of the interior design industry. In a similar vein, she was a participant in the first Ecological Showcase House in Los Angeles.

Q&A
more about suzanne

WHAT PERSONAL INDULGENCE DOES SUZANNE SPEND THE MOST MONEY ON?

A woman of many interests, Suzanne refuses to pick a favorite extravagance. "I like to have an open mind and follow what inspires me at the time" she says. She will admit, however, to a particular passion for traveling the globe and exploring the lifestyles and cultures of other countries. Her travels often guide her creativity.

WHAT COLOR BEST DESCRIBES HER AND WHY?

Strong and vibrant, turquoise most reflects Suzanne's nature.

WHAT OTHER PUBLICATIONS HAVE FEATURED HER WORK?

Suzanne's projects have been published in numerous magazines and tabletop books, most recently *Los Angeles Magazine, Elle Decor* and *California Homes.* Additionally, she appeared on HGTV's *Designers' Challenge,* in an episode that continues in rotation, Chris Lowell's *Interior Motives* and *Malibu Lifestyles,* featuring beach home design. She has written articles for the *Los Angeles Times* and *The Beverly Hills Courier.*

Suzanne Furst Interiors
Suzanne Furst, ASID, CID
8954 West Pico Boulevard, Suite A
Los Angeles, CA 90035
310.275.8077
www.suzannefurstinteriors.com

cheryl**gardner**
CHERYL GARDNER INTERIOR DESIGN

Out of the box. Over the top. Beyond imagination. Such are the phrases Cheryl Gardner's clients use to describe the award-winning interior designer's work.

And one look at her eye-popping interiors reveals they are right. Whether it's a Moroccan-inspired luxury suite on Rodeo Drive for the Academy Awards, art deco glam for a Minnesota condo, charming warmth in a Spanish-style bungalow, or a makeover for a rustic lakeside cabin, the work of Cheryl Gardner Interior Design exemplifies boundless creativity. Her passion for life and for transforming her clients' desires and personalities into unique and personal rooms that are both spectacular to look at and easy to live in emanates in every window treatment, each piece of furniture, and all of the carefully selected accessories.

ABOVE
Entry way of high-end condo with laser cut marble and granite custom design. Anigre wood paneling with cherry and walnut accents. Stainless steel custom console attached to wall.
Photograph by Jeff Johnson Photography

LEFT
Bathroom area of "Man's Retreat" off the master suite. The "Man's Retreat" consists of the master bathroom, office area, work out area and patio all off the master bedroom. Pacific Palisades, CA.
Photograph by Michael Kalla Photography

Cheryl has more than 25 years of experience designing for residential and commercial clients. With New York roots and offices in Los Angeles and Minneapolis, Minnesota, her design firm has clients on both coasts and everywhere in between and offers a full range of expertise, from working as part of a team with a builder and/or architect on new construction, renovation, or remodeling to completing the interior of an existing space — bringing to every job professionalism and enthusiasm. Her designs have been features in numerous publications, including *Architectural Digest, Better Homes and Gardens, California Homes, Los Angeles* magazine, and, most recently, in the *Los Angeles Times, Esquire, Robb Report Luxury Home* magazine, and *LA Home & Décor.*

When she's not working for her clients, Cheryl is serving her community. She was co-chair of DIFFA's (Design Industries Foundation Fighting AIDS) national fundraiser, which debuted in Los Angeles. Additionally, as an active member of the L.A. Chapter of ASID, where she served on the board of directors as membership chair in 2004 and 2005, she is currently head of an outreach program dedicated to helping inner-city kids.

FACING PAGE TOP
Outdoor patio of the "Man's Retreat" off the master suite. Pacific Palisades, CA.
Photograph by Michael Kalla Photography

FACING PAGE BOTTOM
Moroccan Fantasy patio created for the 2004 Oscars Luxury Suite at the Luxe Hotel, Rodeo Drive, Beverly Hills, CA.
Photograph by Michael Kalla Photography

TOP RIGHT
Interior of the "Ultimate Garage for the Modern Man" for the 2004 Esquire Design House. Beverly Hills, CA.
Photograph by Michael Kalla Photography

BOTTOM RIGHT
The night shot of the "Ultimate Garage for the Modern Man" for the 2004 esquire design house. Beverly Hills, CA.
Photograph by Michael Kalla Photography

ABOVE & INSET
Traditional bathroom remodel with custom mahogany cabinetry, granite countertops and floor with
metal insets. 7,500-square-foot residence, Claremont, CA.
Photographs by Michael Kalla Photography

FACING PAGE TOP
Art Deco/Moderne dining room of high-end condo mixes reproductions and antiques.
Photograph by Jeff Johnson Photography

FACING PAGE BOTTOM
Art Deco/Moderne master bedroom of high end condo mixes reproductions and antiques.
Photograph by Jeff Johnson Photography

more about cheryl

WHAT IS THE MOST UNUSUAL PROJECT SHE'S EVER WORKED ON?

Cheryl created the ultimate fantasy garage for The 2004 Esquire House, designed by architect Richard Landy. "When they first handed it to me, I asked myself, 'What am I going to do with a garage?'." What she did, however, was create an automotive-inspired retreat that was masculine, sexy, and cool. With six plasma TVs, car paint on the walls, a stamped stainless steel floor, sofas made from the back seats of the Chrysler 300C, a backlit glass bar with the look of a smashed windshield, and a chandelier resembling a tire, it is a true testosterone-fueled hideout.

WHAT COLOR BEST DESCRIBES HER AND WHY?

The veteran designer is an energetic woman. Vibrant, dramatic colors like red and violet reflect her intense personality.

Cheryl Gardner Interior Design
Cheryl Gardner, ASID, CID
569 North Rossmore Avenue, Suite 310
Los Angeles, CA 90004
323.856.0812
www.cherylgardner.com

greystone**mansion**

LEFT & RIGHT
Greystone Mansion.
Photographs by Mary E. Nichols

Many hail Greystone Mansion as one of the grandest homes on the West Coast. Arguably the largest and most dramatic house ever built in Beverly Hills, the manse was designed by renowned Southern California architect Gordon B. Kaufman. A splendid English Gothic Revival structure named for its somber gray appearance, the manor comprises more than 46,000 square feet of living space in 55 rooms. And since 2002, it has also been home to the annual Beverly Hills Garden & Design Showcase.

The City of Beverly Hills purchased the famed Greystone Estate in 1965 for $1.3 million (far less than the 1928 price tag of $3.2 million). Though the grounds were dedicated as a public park in 1971 and the estate was named to the Register of Historic Places in 1976, the entirety was sorely neglected for decades and slowly fell into disrepair, says Steve Miller, Director of the Beverly Hills Community Services Department. After 30 years, however, the city turned its attention to what Steve calls "a hidden treasure sitting in our backyard" and began to invest in its restoration. The Showcase is part of that effort.

A longtime favorite location for movie makers, scenes from films such as *Indecent Proposal, What Women Want, The Witches of Eastwick, Town & Country*, and, most recently, *Garfield 2* have been shot at Greystone. In recent years, the city has held boutique-type events to reacquaint members of the community with Greystone Park and Mansion, Steve says. Theater productions, afternoon tea, children's art camps, concerts, and the like have drawn a wide audience, and a $4.5 million garden restoration (with one final phase in the works) has earned the grounds a reputation as a worthy setting for weddings — even those of celebrities such as Kirk Douglas.

Says Steve, "Little by little we've been trying to provide opportunities for residents to experience the majesty of a way of life that's, in some way, long gone. It's part of the early days of Hollywood and the history of the city. We want people everywhere to know of this special treasure." In its short life, the Showcase has become a big part of that.

Held each November and now in its fifth year, the event is produced in conjunction with the American Society of Interior Designers, Los Angeles Chapter, whose members are enlisted to return the estate to its 1920's grandeur. Top-notch designers fill empty rooms and hallways with color, furnishings, drapery treatments, art, and accessories. With their skill and artistry they give visitors to the home a taste of how the original residents, the prominent Doheny family, lived. Or, as Steve puts it: "They take an empty shell that has this cold, eerie silence and bring it to life. If you see it before and after, it just takes you aback."

FACING PAGE
Designed by Darrell Schmitt, ASID.
Photograph by Mary E. Nichols

TOP RIGHT
Designed by Anne Wait, ASID.
Photograph by Mary E. Nichols

BOTTOM RIGHT
Designed by Suzanne Furst, ASID.
Photograph by Mary E. Nichols

ABOVE
Designed by Kathleen Beall, ASID.
Photograph by Mary E. Nichols

FACING PAGE TOP
Designed by Jean Zinner, ASID.
Photograph by Mary E. Nichols

FACING PAGE BOTTOM
Designed by Helene Lotto, Allied Member ASID and Fernando Diaz, ASID.
Photograph by Mary E. Nichols

Year after year, the thrill is in seeing an entirely different interpretation of the same spaces, says Sybil J.B. van Dijs, current president of ASID, L.A. Chapter. But the challenge is in creating a seamless interior. The goal, Sybil says, is for the mansion to feel as if only one person designed it — which with nearly two dozen participating designers putting their particular spin on '20s luxe, is no easy feat. To start, designers incorporate today's color palates while taking cues from yesteryear on things such as furniture and decorative accessory placement. A committee reviewed and approved each designer's ideas before that designer can bring his or her vision to life.

Though designers spend their own money to participate and the project requires hundreds of hours to plan and execute, not to mention a commitment to be onsite during the days that the public is touring, competition is fierce and interest comes from all around the L.A. area and Southern California. To be selected as a participant is a highly coveted honor, says Sybil, who in 2005 designed the Showcase living room.

"It's an incredible venture," she says. And as the 4,500 visitors last year can attest, the results are equally stunning.

Greystone Park & Mansion
City of Beverly Hills
905 Loma Vista Drive
Beverly Hills, CA 90210
310.550.4796

tina**levinson**

LEFT
Inviting and warm upstairs landing features a sitting and study area. Custom wood computer equipment seamlessly integrates the technology. Elegant window treatments highlight the lake views.
Photograph by Peter Christiansen Valli

RIGHT
Artwork by Kelly Viss. Custom bar with leather upholstered doors and nail head trim.
Photograph by Peter Christiansen Valli

t's not unusual for clients of Haven Home Furnishings to spend an afternoon at the store, sipping coffee, hanging out, and working with the interior designers on staff. The elegant, casual Westlake Village showroom offers a variety of style, era, and quality options, making it a welcoming destination for new as well as established homeowners.

Brimming with unique luxury goods — furniture, bedding, and accessories — and staffed with a team of talented designers, the 8-year-old boutique offers a no-nonsense approach to interior design combined with boundless creativity and energy. The sales floor is continuously refreshed with new products and fresh ideas. The back room and warehouse is a treasure trove of flea market finds, estate sale purchases, and other wonderful accent pieces.

Available for as little as advice on a new sofa and as much as a total interior overhaul, the store's designers help clients narrow their selections from myriad options and design to reflect each homeowner's lifestyle and personality. The process often starts with an in-home consultation to gather input for creating beautiful, functional decorating solutions. Haven team members then help clients navigate the design process, from bare walls down to the last accessory, with patience, understanding, and confidence.

Haven Home Furnishings
Tina Levinson
2886 Thousand Oaks Boulevard
Thousand Oaks, CA 91362
805.374.9060

helene**lotto**

F or more than 23 years, Helene Lotto has put together hundreds of homes and has provided interior design services to many clients throughout Southern California, Las Vegas, Chicago, and New York City. If there is one thing to be said about her approach, it's that she takes interior design very seriously.

The Lotto Design Group is a full-service interior design firm specializing in all aspects of design for small and extremely large projects. Helene is a California Certified interior designer, an Allied member of the American Society of Interior Designer, and a professional member of the National Kitchen & Bath Association. She works with a team of design professionals and CAD draftsmen who are on staff and have a degree or certification in their specialty. Vicki Korniski, NKBA, is a full-time kitchen and bath designer with an impressive reputation for creating beautiful, functional kitchens and baths.

Prior to becoming a professional designer, Helene planned to be a commercial artist but marriage came first. Then, she and her husband moved from New York City to California, where she opened an art gallery, selling to interior designers and eventually taking on some decorating projects herself. Shortly after, she attended UCLA and graduated with a Certificate of Environmental Interior Design.

LEFT
The Italian Bar is a reproduction of one seen in Italy by the client. It is the focal point of the room.
Photograph by David Kessler Studios

That was more than two decades ago, and as the years marched on, the realm of interior design did, too. "Before the MGM Grand fire in Las Vegas in the '70s, there wasn't the testing of fabrics. After the terrible loss of life, codes and regulations came into effect. If something looked good, it just wasn't enough." Helene says.

Today, however, interior design means more than choosing fabrics, flooring, and other accessories for clients. Designers are not only responsible for specifying materials but also for the implication of their designs, she says. "We are charged with the health, safety, and welfare of the public. Codes and regulations are constantly changing, and there's so much more responsibility than people can even imagine."

One of the leading interior design firms in California, The Lotto Design Group works as a team to transform residential and commercial spaces into warm, welcoming showplaces. Some of Helene's awards include a Presidential Citation and the Edna O'Brien Award for Distinguished Service from the L. A. Chapter of ASID. She was honored for distinguished service to the City of Beverly Hills as well.

Though she does keep an eye on the latest trends, Helene prefers classic elegance in the Old-World tradition. That's not to say she can't accommodate those who want a more contemporary interior, as her team prides itself on listening well and interpreting the wants and needs of their clients. "The client and project come first, before any other considerations," Helene says.

What is abundantly clear is the passion she has for her work, which is, in reality, more like a devotion to providing her clients with magnificent rooms that are tailored to their desires and needs. Helene enjoys space planning, problem solving, and even

the business aspect of interior design. "It's always new and exciting to me," she says, her enthusiasm evident in her voice. "It's a new experience every day. I've tried so many things in my life, but nothing completes me the way that design does."

The best part? Her clients' joy when their projects are finished and they go home at the end of each day to a space that reflects their specifics tastes and lifestyles. "When I get a call or an e-mail telling me how much they love it or how I've impacted their lives," Helene says, "I am reminded why I'm an interior designer. What greater satisfaction than to know you can improve someone's lifestyle?" she asks. "It's what we hope to achieve."

LEFT
The columns and arch were added to the master bathroom to create continuity with the rest of the Mediterranean home.
Photograph by Mark Lohman

FACING PAGE
Colors of red and gold were used to create this space. A soft ragging of both colors on the walls make this Old World room both inviting and comfortable.
Photograph by Mark Lohman

Q&A
more about helene

WHO HAS HAD THE BIGGEST INFLUENCE ON HER CAREER?

While in college, Helene had a professor of decorative arts who opened up a world of design and possibilities to the budding young designer.

WHAT DOES SHE LIKE MOST ABOUT DOING BUSINESS IN SOUTHERN CALIFORNIA?

The mild and consistent climate allows interior designers to experiment with new materials and technologies both in the interior as well as exterior spaces. Clients are more open to change being that there are so many creative people in the area working in the entertainment industry. California is the trendsetter in new designs.

The Lotto Design Group
Helene Lotto, Allied Member, ASID, CID, NKBA
31324 Via Colinas, Suite 114
Westlake Village, CA 91362
818.879.6183
www.helenelotto.com

michael**martinez**

MICHAEL MARTINEZ INTERIOR DESIGN

Michael Martinez is a client-centric designer. The people who hire him, above all else, have shaped his 25-year career, giving him inspiration and helping propel him to the top of his profession. His business has grown through reputation and word of mouth, as clients pay him the greatest possible compliment when they ask him to design a second or third home and they suggest his work to their friends and family. "That's success," he says.

With a warm, friendly manner and an obvious zest for life, the Southern California native takes a gentle approach with every new client. Realizing that the interior design process can be overwhelming and can stir up emotions in a homeowner, Michael listens carefully to clients' desires, paying attention to even the unspoken and infusing fun and excitement into each step of a project. "Hiring an interior designer is such a personal decision," he says. "You should really feel comfortable with that person."

Setting ego aside, Michael bases his designs on his clients' lifestyles and tastes. "This is not about me or my style. This is a collaborative effort, and, in the end, the decisions are always the client's to make," he says. "I love being able to mold a home from concept to reality, knowing that I am doing something that the client will not only live in but also enjoy and treasure every day."

Each job begins with a clean slate and is as individual as the space itself. That way, Michael says, when the work is done, it reflects the homeowner's experiences and preferences. Always, the designer's goal is to leave a client with a personalized environment that charms and delights them. And judging by the number of referrals he's received through the years, he does just that. "A satisfied client will always refer you," he says.

Q&A
more about michael

WHAT ONE THING WOULD HE DO TO GIVE NEW LIFE TO A DULL HOUSE?

Color adds energy and attitude, Michael says, be it painting a wall, hanging richly hued draperies, or bringing in vibrant accessories.

YOU WOULDN'T GUESS IT, BUT MICHAEL'S FRIENDS WOULD TELL YOU THAT HE IS ...

A chocoholic (Leonidas is his favorite) and a true romantic.

WHAT DOES HE LIKE MOST ABOUT DOING BUSINESS IN SOUTHERN CALIFORNIA?

The weather can't be beat, and that makes interior design easier, he says, since there are not extreme seasons to consider, there is a lot more freedom when determining the direction of the design.

Michael Martinez Interior Design
Michael Martinez
2317 N. Gower Street
Los Angeles, CA 90068
Los Angeles 323.461.9111
Palm Springs 760.327.9111

carolyn**e.oliver**

OLIVER'S *A DESIGN STUDIO*

Elsie de Wolfe once said, "Taste is a compass that never errs." It's a tenant by which Carolyn Oliver lives her life and runs her design business.

A woman of exquisite style, Carolyn opened a home décor store, Oliver's, in Pasadena's historic Theatre District 11 years ago, after leaving her post as the first woman executive director of Los Angeles's Junior Chamber of Commerce. Soon, customers would ask for help with their decorating projects, and Carolyn began to apply her education and experience in the visual arts to a new passion: interior design.

In a short time, Oliver's has garnered a reputation for success. Carolyn was chosen by the L.A. County Museum of Art to assist in the creation of its retail venue home shop, she has been selected the last six years to participate in the Pasadena Showcase for the Arts (the nation's largest home and garden tour), as well as in the L.A. Assistance League of Southern California Design House. Additionally, her work has appeared on PBS's *Find!* and CBS's *Beautiful Homes and Great Estates* and in *Elle Décor, LA Magazine, Kitchen & Bath Design News*, and the newly released *Designer Showcase Book*, published by Schiffer.

LEFT
Oliver and GMS Construction transformed a large walk-in closet into an intimate guest quarters dining area by creating openings in two walls and replicating the original iron work in this architecturally significant Pasadena Estate.
Photograph by Alex Vertikoff

Carolyn attributes her success to her geologist father, who instilled in her a love of art and the importance of lifelong learning and personal growth. "When I was young, he told me that you could lose everything except your knowledge and love of learning," she remembers. In the second grade, her parents enrolled her in private art lessons that continued until her university work began in Florence, Italy.

Known for her artistry in residential design and her proven track record of capturing the essence of her international clientele and their individual lifestyles, Carolyn draws on her art background for her interior design work. "What separates a good designer from a great designer is sustainability and proportions that are as perfect as in the finest museum painting," she says. "To create perfectly proportioned, suitable rooms where my clients are surrounded by the objects that really make them happy" is the overriding goal in every project.

ABOVE LEFT
The 1931 hacienda dining room by esteemed Pasadena architect Wallace Neff is one of Oliver's favorites. She found large scale antique water colors to flank the doorway, custom lighting, and a subtle wall design that serve only as a backdrop for the incredible view of the entire valley.
Photograph by Peter Christiansen Valli

ABOVE RIGHT
Oliver's lifelong love affair with Italy began as a young woman when she began her university studies in Florence. Her love of working with stone is apparent in the custom-designed mosaic floor and the transformation of this 1910 outdoor porch into a lovely haven for quiet reflection.
Photograph by Peter Christiansen Valli

FACING PAGE
Inspired by the Estate's classical Beaux Arts architectural style Oliver used simple Greek and Roman forms and took a cue from the Pompeii runs to select the plethora of stone tile, color palette, and accessories.
Photograph by Peter Christiansen Valli

Q&A

more about carolyn

WHAT IS SOMETHING MOST PEOPLE DON'T KNOW ABOUT HER?

Carolyn grew up on a horse farm in Kentucky, where she still likes to go fishing with her brother, Charlie.

WHAT PERSONAL INDULGENCE DOES CAROLYN SPEND THE MOST MONEY ON?

"In this business it is so easy to give and give of yourself," Carolyn says. She's found that working out with my personal trainer, Anita Pressman, several times a week restores her physical, mental, and spiritual balance. "It's paramount in keeping me 100 percent."

Photograph by Martin Ledford

greg**parker**

PARKER WEST INTERIORS

LEFT
This room was inspired by the French Art Deco period. Furnishings have clean yet elegant lines and incorporate exotic veneers and rich fabric textures.
Photograph by Alexander Vertikoff

RIGHT
The clear piano gives a fantastic lift to the room. It blends easily with the mirrored console and Lalique sconces.
Photograph by Alexander Vertikoff

If there is one thing to be said about Greg Parker, it's that he doesn't follow the rules. Though he describes himself as a traditionalist, he's not afraid to take risks and push his designs a little further than one might expect. "Outside of the box," he says, "is always how I will approach a project."

Perhaps one reason the 50-year-old California native comes at his work from a different angle is that he came to the business a little later than most — 13 years ago — after a successful music career. With graduate degrees in piano and voice from the Peabody Conservatory of Music (now the Peabody Institute of John Hopkins University) and stints singing with opera companies in Baltimore and Philadelphia behind him, Greg returned to L.A. to be closer to his family.

It was then that he decided to concentrate on the design side of his artistic nature. And though he still composes and arranges music, much of his creative energy is spent creating unique and detailed interiors for his clients. "There are many parallels between design and music," Greg explains. "The concepts of harmony, balance, rhythm, and line flow back and forth one to the other."

With a small, dedicated team, Parker West Interiors places a premium on a collaborative relationship between homeowner and designer, and the firm tends to attract clients who feel the same way. Through this process, Greg is able to refine and tailor each client's vision to spectacular result, blending old and new elements and giving each space timeless appeal but with a definitive edge.

What might that edge include? "I am really interested in different kinds of materials and how they can be used in untraditional ways." One can use glass in a backsplash, or a recycled paper countertop, or fiberoptics in a stair rail. "It takes only a little twist to make a design intriguing and give a client something that's beyond what they hoped for."

ABOVE LEFT
The wine room incorporates fiber optic lighting in the domed star ceiling and the art glass panel. It is opulent and functional.
Photograph by Alexander Vertikoff

ABOVE RIGHT
An elegantly informal dining room mixes traditional furniture with texture and eastern accents.
Photograph by Alexander Vertikoff

FACING PAGE
The geometry of a space can result in a dynamic, energetic room. Materials include different marble countertops, alder and walnut cabinetry, copper, and stainless steel.
Photograph by Alexander Vertikoff

Q&A
more about greg

IF HE COULD ELIMINATE ONE ARCHITECTURAL STYLE FROM THE WORLD, WHAT WOULD THAT BE?

The overbuilt McMansions that have flooded the American landscape are eyesores, he says.

WHAT COLOR BEST DESCRIBES GREG AND WHY?

Greg says that green is the shade that represents him most closely. Organic and natural, it's associated with gardens and the outdoors, both things that the designer loves.

HOW DO GREG'S FRIENDS DESCRIBE HIM?

They say he's a kind, big-hearted man who is generous to a fault.

WHAT ONE THING WOULD HE DO TO GIVE NEW LIFE TO A DULL HOUSE?

A good lighting plan is essential, he says.

Parker West Interiors
Greg Parker
1036 Marengo Avenue
South Pasadena, CA 91030
626.403.5008
www.parkerwestinteriros.com

pasadena**showcase**

HOUSE OF DESIGN

LEFT & RIGHT
2005 Pasadena Showcase House.
Photographs by Alex Vertikoff

W hat do you get when you take a 10,000-square-foot estate, 20-plus interior design firms, and tens of thousands of visitors willing to pay $25 to $30 each for a walkthrough? Beautiful music, that's what.

Each spring for the last 41 years, the nonprofit Pasadena Showcase House for the Arts produces the highly acclaimed Pasadena Showcase House of Design to benefit the Los Angeles Philharmonic and children's music education programs. One of the oldest and largest projects of its kind in the United States, the event features the creations of the top home and garden designers in the L.A. area and has resulted in cumulative donations of more than $14 million to the symphony, schools, and other local organizations. In 2005, "The success of the Pasadena Showcase House of Design enabled the Pasadena Showcase House for the Arts to award $700,000 in gifts and grants to 36 organizations benefiting music education and the arts," says Chairman Jennifer Walston Johnson.

With the considerable talents of hundreds of Southern California's leading interior and exterior design professionals, a different house is transformed each year into a captivating exhibit of the latest concepts. The 2005 Showcase House, designed by the world-renowned Architect to the Stars, Wallace Neff, and built in 1929, is an elegant Italian Revival-style estate sitting on more than two lush acres. The house and its grounds were meticulously restored to their original splendor and adapted to the 21st century with cutting-edge comforts and innovations.

After the advisory committee selected a color palette for the house — warm neutrals; earthy golds, browns, and oranges; muted greens, blues, and grays; and terra cotta and red — designers went to work, putting their creativity to the test in their assigned spaces. The results were a stunning combination of traditional and modern, blending the past and future in a dynamic and stylish way — and with an exotic flare that delighted visitors.

John Cole's dining room celebrated the grand Mediterranean splendor of the handsomely appointed manse. With shades of brown and apricot, appetizing fabrics and wall coverings, and French tapestry, he brought a rich ambiance to the space. Combining distressed woods with marble, stone, and gold-leafing generates an elegant style for gracious dining, he says.

The master suite, always a visitor favorite, fell to David Reaume Construction & Design. Updated with dreamy amenities, the traditionally styled rooms boast a quiet symmetry with striking Baccarat chandeliers, a neutral color scheme, his and hers closets, and a fireplace with a stone surround in the bedroom; and floor-to-ceiling glass tiles, a travertine floor, and platinum-finished plumbing fixtures in the bath. "With every detail beautifully addressed, the homeowners will find the master bedroom suite difficult to leave each day," Reaume says.

Technology meets serenity in the grandparent's suite. Saxony's Street's Sue Potter gave the rooms a luxurious look and feel with Nancy Corzine's latest and soft colors and fabrics, then she packed in the latest electronic equipment, including a flat-screen television, a laptop, and a state-of-the-art sound system — all tastefully placed so as not to disturb the quiet repose.

ABOVE LEFT
Designed by Caroline Baker, Allied Member, ASID, 2004 Showcase House.
Photograph by Alex Vertikoff

ABOVE RIGHT
Designed by Carolyn Oliver.
Photograph by Peter Christiansen Valli

FACING PAGE TOP LEFT
Designed by Jennifer Bevan-Montoya, ASID, CID.
Photograph by Alex Vertikoff

FACING PAGE BOTTOM LEFT
Designed by Greg Parker.
Photograph by Alex Vertikoff

The inspiration for Jerome Thiebault's and Laurent Pingault's media room was "a sophisticated world traveler who has brought home treasures from foreign lands," the designers say. An expansive space, the Roche Bobois colleagues gave the room a contemporary flair with two distinct seating areas and a bar.

Other designers who participated in the Pasadena Showcase House of Design whose work can be seen in this publication include Greg Parker of Parker West, Carolyn Oliver, Jennifer Bevan-Montoya, and Caroline Baker.

"While Showcase provides an opportunity for designers to reach a wide audience, it represents a huge commitment of their time, energy and resources," Jennifer Walston Johnson says. "Without the designers there would be no showcase house. Our organization is so appreciative of their efforts on behalf of the project."

FACING PAGE TOP
Designed by David Reaume.
Photograph by Scott Bradford

FACING PAGE BOTTOM
Designed by John Cole.
Photograph by Peter Christiansen Valli

TOP RIGHT
Designed by Jerome Thiebault and Laurent Pingault.
Photograph by Vicken Sahakian

BOTTOM RIGHT
Designed by Sue Potter, Allied Member, ASID, Associate IIDA.
Photograph by Alex Vertikoff

Pasadena Showcase House of Design
P.O. Box 80262
San Marino, CA 91118
www.pasadenashowcase.org

cynthia**piana**
& lori**souza**

PIANA DESIGN

Piana Design is fast emerging as one of the hottest interior design firms in California. Partners Cynthia Piana and Lori Souza, combine a love of architecture and design with extensive experience in construction and project management. They are experts at providing their clients stylistic and beautiful custom living spaces efficiently and quickly — with a special personal touch. Many of their projects are within the state, ranging from the Bay Area to Orange County, they are frequently called upon to work in other states and abroad.

Several characteristics make Piana Design unique within the art of interior design: Construction expertise and collaboration with builders and architects allow them to enter a project in the initial stages and implement innovative as well as cost-effective ideas. Additionally, both travel the globe searching for emerging trends, the finest materials and products, and new and innovative ideas to incorporate into their creations.

Never women to conform to convention, Cynthia and Lori say that breaking the rules is part of the fun with their job. Their favorite projects are those in which they have the creative freedom to define clients' tastes in new ways. For them, the joy in interior design comes from pushing the limits and delivering ideas that exceed clients' imaginations.

Mixing elements of today to create a 14-foot island in a Spanish-style kitchen, they sourced tiles from Spain and had the tiles inset in turquoise-colored concrete

LEFT
This exquisite 1860's table, imported directly from Spain, over looks the breathtaking Laguna Beach sunset. As one dines, he is greeted by the soft sea breeze and the temperate sounds of the calming waves.
Photograph by Peter Christiansen Valli

— something neither their client nor the fabricator had ever seen. For another client, they searched for months to discover master bedroom furniture, finally finding a bed they liked in a museum and having it re-created. And when the owners of a 1920's Colonial home in Hancock Park wanted a touch of Nantucket, Cynthia and Lori built a ship in the couple's 2-year-old son's bedroom.

With matching sunny dispositions and optimism to spare, the gifted women make a great team: Cynthia thinks of the big picture; Lori likes the details. Cynthia enjoys the serious side of business; Lori keeps things light. Cynthia relishes presenting their ideas to clients; Lori goes to great lengths to define a well planned work space or room. Together, they are always up for the challenge of creating fresh, dramatic designs. And they are always up for a good time.

If clients constantly remark that the pair looks like they are having fun, that's because they are. They are business partners and friends who get to create outside of the norm. Both are passionate about what they do and find interior design more good time than hard work.

TOP LEFT
The theatre-deep sofa is an extensive custom mix of plush leather and vintage fabrics. The acclaimed Mexican artist, Miguel Ramirez, was commissioned to paint the four bull fighters and conceal three high tech plasma screens.
Photograph by Peter Christiansen Valli

BOTTOM LEFT
The master bed was inspired by the 19th century Gothic Revival, that was originally destined for the White House. Nagenan red burn out, Moorish pattern fabric adorns the bed post as Piana's mix of the Anichini bedding brings a fresh perspective and is beset by salida del sol walls.
Photograph by Peter Christiansen Valli

FACING PAGE
A fusion of custom handmade tile flown in from Spain, inset into a vibrant turquoise concrete island. The Navajo Sunset Venetian plaster walls create the backdrop for the warm South American welcome, as inspired by the client's cultural background. The inscription, set above the windows, invites that the kitchen is the heart of the home.
Photograph by Peter Christiansen Valli

Q&A
more about cynthia & lori

WHAT PERSONAL INDULGENCE DO YOU SPEND THE MOST MONEY ON?

Undeniable clotheshorses and shoe aficionados, both women put the same kind of time and energy (not to mention cash!) into creating fabulous outfits as they do designing beautiful rooms.

WHAT ONE ELEMENT OF STYLE OR PHILOSOPHY HAVE YOU STUCK WITH FOR YEARS THAT STILL WORK FOR YOU TODAY?

Cynthia: "Have integrity; deliver what you say and on time."

Lori: "Let the clients do most of the talking."

WHAT IS THE SINGLE THING YOU WOULD DO TO BRING A DULL HOUSE TO LIFE?

Cynthia: "Add color for warmth — amazingly easy yet incredible results."

Lori: "Use beutiful artwork as your focal point."

WHAT IS THE BEST PART OF BEING AN INTERIOR DESIGNER?

The endless amount of research, learning, traveling and meeting with new clientele and I get to wear fabulous clothes!

Piana Design
Cynthia Piana, ASID, IDS, NKBA, WFHA
Lori Souza
26027 Huntington Lane, Suite C
Valencia, CA 91355
661.702.9490
www.pianadesign.com

suepotter

SAXONY STREET, INC.

Classy and comfortable with a California accent — that's what Saxony Street is known for throughout the Los Angeles area. For nearly 20 years, this philosophy has pleased many local clients and spilled over to Las Vegas and Hawaii, as well. Now, Sue Potter, founder and CEO of Saxony Street, is enthusiastically looking forward to being able to work with more clients through the expanded services her firm offers.

Supported by designer Ryan-Gordon Jackson and staff, Sue has added architectural services to her portfolio. This is due partly to the continuing growth of home remodeling and expansion in Southern California and her observation that clients prefer the ease and convenience of dealing with a design firm that can serve them every step of the way, from conception through the completion of a project. She believes this is the only way to ensure that the integrity of the vision is carried through correctly and creatively in order to produce the most satisfying results — because function and beauty don't just happen!

Working from a studio in charming Valley Village, Sue and associates continue to bring their expertise to a variety of upscale residential and selective commercial design projects. Part of the secret of Saxony Street's success through the years has been the ability to listen. Knowing what makes the client happy gives the

ABOVE
This chic bathroom encompasses his and hers sinks as well as a woman's vanity and a luxurious spa shower. A striking mosaic in the room frames the handmade, clear blue crackle tile and shows off the deco-inspired, black bronze bath fixtures.
Photograph by Peter Christiansen Valli

LEFT
This formal living room was inspired by the client's desire for classic elegance. The custom-designed stone fireplace is the focal point for the symmetrical seating arrangement while a combination of silks, velvets, and gorgeous brocades provide texture and excitement to sumptuous furnishings.
Photograph by Martin Fine

designers a better understanding of where to start and how to best make the clients part of the process. Sue, who describes herself as a people-pleaser, is happy only when her clients are happy.

Her flexible Gemini nature allows her to change direction in short order and gives her the confidence to take creative risks without fear of failing. And her type-A personality means she has the tenacity to keep at it until the final picture is hung and the last pillow is plumped to the client's total satisfaction. She says that the very best part of her job is to see the joy on clients' faces when they see their completed projects.

Sue's own home is a manifestation of her personal evolution. It incorporates a mix of styles but has the overall feel of Art Deco, a period that's always held special appeal for her. Recently, after working with a client who had lived in Japan and

wanted an authentic Japanese feel brought into their home, she turned her eye toward an Asian style. Sue's home office, where she often works at off hours in the company of her three cats, showcases her newfound appreciation of this simple and beautiful design. Being open to the old and the new, is the best way to keep creative thinking always fresh.

ABOVE
Rustic furnishings, rich woods, and Asian antiques tie the contemporary architecture of this beach house to the clients' desire for a comfortable, cozy retreat.
Photograph by Steve Brinkman

FACING PAGE LEFT
This opulent Italianate powder bathroom was refurbished for the Pasadena Showcase House 2002.
Photograph by David Valenzuela

FACING PAGE RIGHT
The seven-foot tall iron crystal chandelier hanging from the rotunda unites the first and second floors of this fantastic Mediterranean estate.
Photograph by Martin Fine

Q&A

more about sue

WHAT IS THE MOST UNUSUAL PROJECT SHE'S WORKED ON?

Sue once transformed an extra bedroom into a library with a hidden safe closet and a
7-foot-long, three-level custom tank with all the amenities for the family's pet iguana.

**WHAT PERSONAL INDULGENCE DOES SHE SPEND THE MOST
MONEY ON?**

Shoes, handbags, time at the salon, and spa treatments.

WHAT IS THE BEST PART OF BEING AN INTERIOR DESIGNER?

The look on the client's face when seeing the project complete.

Saxony Street, Inc.
Sue Potter, Allied Member, ASID,
Associate, IIDA
11659 Riverside Drive
Valley Village, CA 91601
818.623.8001
www.saxonystreet.com

valeriepugliese

DESIGNS BY VALERIE

With her first-ever interior design project, Valerie Pugliese burst onto the scene. Her fairytale-themed bedroom and bath for the House for Hope Design Showcase, in the gated Lake Sherwood community, was a hit that had guests telling their friends and reaching for their wallets.

Ten thousand people viewed her work in the five weeks that the $6 million house was open for tours. Editors at *Romantic Homes* magazine saw the room and decided to do a feature story on it. And a one-of-a-kind desk/vanity sold the first day. The piece, which Valerie found at a flea market and decoupaged with pictures of roses, seemed like a bit of a risk, given the stately Old World style of the house, but it was a crowd-pleaser: Dozens of guests wanted to purchase it. An amateur photographer, Valerie also sold several photos she'd taken of castles in England and Ireland, an achievement the young designer says was almost as exciting as being asked to participate in the showhouse.

A former assistant designer for the Lake Sherwood Development, Valerie began her career as an interior designer four years ago at the urging of her husband, whom she says is her biggest fan. In business for herself just a year, Valerie's proudest works to date are the Sherwood rooms. And it's easy to see why.

Though the bedroom is for a young girl and centers on a palette of rosy pink, it's not overly girly. It is a feminine, elegant space in which a woman of any age could feel comfortable. Muralist Don Noble's hand-painted castles are a spectacular focal point.

Interior design not only allows Valerie to fulfil her career dreams, it also lets her help those who are less fortunate. The Lake Sherwood house raised money for the Wellness Community, an organization that provides support to cancer patients and their families. Through her affiliation with the Interior Design Society, she does other charitable work as well, including a project that assists wayward teenage girls and an event that generated $3,000 for the Coalition to End Family Violence.

ABOVE
The client wanted a whole new look the only thing that stayed were the cabinets which we stained a dark espresso to go with the mosaic glass back splash.
Photograph by Peter Christiansen Valli

RIGHT
The new spa tub was a much-needed feature. We used the same mosaic glass back splash and added some framed florals to give the room that "outside in the woods" feel.
Photograph by Peter Christiansen Valli

FACING PAGE
This master bedroom was featured in a showcase tour for the holidays. We were going for a warm and cozy feeling, which I think we achieved by using a rich brown paint on the walls.
Photograph by Peter Christiansen Valli

quentin**rance**

QUENTIN RANCE ENTERPRISES, INC.

LEFT & RIGHT
In producing the Spanish style interior, the request was to bring the exterior 1000
-square-foot covered patio into the main part of the house creating a 2000-square-
foot great room. The forming of a two-sided adobe central fireplace was the focal
point of this room. The surrounding area was fragmented into specific spaces which
were all color coordinated. These included the sitting room, the breakfast room, the
media room, the bar and the music room.
Photographs by Peter Christiansen Valli

Quentin Rance has been fortunate to have traveled extensively throughout the world, and he uses the wealth of knowledge gleaned on his trips to create exciting interiors.

In executing contracts within the Greek Isles, the South of France, Switzerland, Ireland, England, and North America, he has shown the ability to translate his clients' wishes into homes that reflect their image. In doing so, he has still created the excitment one would expect from an interior designer of his experience. From traditional to transitional, high-tech to contemporary, Quentin is always at home with his task. A Lake Arrowhead Swiss-style mountain chalet, a Tudor home down to the last detail, and a 157-foot ocean-going yacht are among his many commissions.

Quentin received his training in England, where he established his first company in London. He is a member of the Chartered Society of Designers and was elevated to Fellow status in 1981 for his professional achievements in the United Kingdom. He opened Quentin Rance Enterprises, Inc. in 1982 in Los Angeles, where he was already affiliated with the American Society of Interior Designers. An active and dedicated member, he has served the L. A. Chapter of ASID as an officer in some capacity for the past 23 years.

Quentin Rance Enterprises, Inc.
Quentin Rance, ASID, CID, FCSD
18005 Rancho Street
Encino, CA 91316
818.705.8111

david**reaume**

DAVID REAUME CONSTRUCTION & DESIGN, INC.

LEFT
Creating a warm inviting environment, as in "the great room" of this beautifully built guest house, is the hallmark of a David Reaume project.
Photograph by Martin Fine

RIGHT
Every bath designed by David's company is marked with an individual signature in tile layout and color, and then accentuated with only the finest fixtures.
Photograph by Tom Hinkley

David Reaume has a friendly, easy-going manner that may or may not be the result of his being the youngest of seven children. What is certain, however, is the role that his parents played in their son's career choice. While he was a boy growing up in Pasadena, David's interior designer mother and financial planner father purchased and renovated houses as a hobby, thus planting the seed for his future in construction.

He began building high-end homes in the area in 1988 and quickly rose to the top of his profession. Five years ago David launched the interior design side of his business. It was a natural addition, David says, as he'd already been doing the work unofficially for years. Putting together an interior design team that includes his 82-year-old mother Jacqueline Reaume, senior designer Michele Stone, and Jim

O'Halloran only took his company to the next level. Now, David says, "We are a full-service company with everything under one hat."

Designing and remodeling down-to-earth homes for real people with real lives, David Reaume Construction has a simple approach to approachable interiors: "Bring it back to basics," David says. "We are very traditional and we somehow have a knack for knowing what people want in an everyday situation," he says. Indeed, David's rooms are always the most well-received each year at the Pasadena Showcase House of Design.

Comfort is the driving factor in every project, Michele says, and neutrals are the order of the day. Equally important, she says, is reflecting the personality of the client, who tends to be a person with a more conservative bent, who doesn't crave

wild animal prints or bold wall color. More interested in pleasing the homeowner than making a statement, David wants every room of the houses his company builds and decorates to be so useful and beautiful that each one is a competing favorite — the inviting kitchen, the comfy family room, the cozy bedroom. "I want our clients to love all of the spaces in their homes so much that deciding where to spend their downtime is a difficult task."

ABOVE
The function and beauty exemplified in this Georgian inspired design is why some of the finest homes in California showcase a David Reaume kitchen.
Photograph by Scott Bradford

FACING PAGE TOP
This beautiful bedroom features soft feminine lines paired with neutral colors punctuated by strong accent colors which make it perfect for both husband and wife.
Photograph by Martin Fine

FACING PAGE BOTTOM
Gracious views, an elegant fireplace and a sophisticated color palette make this guest house a perfect home away from home for any visitor.
Photograph by Martin Fine

Q&A
more about david

WHAT ONE THING WOULD HE DO TO GIVE A HOME NEW LIFE?

A kitchen and bath man, David believes that quality cabinetry with a creative finish can take a room from boring to beautiful.

WHAT DOES DAVID ENJOY MOST ABOUT BEING A DESIGNER?

"I love seeing a project through from start to finish. It's very rewarding to see ideas materialize," he says.

WHAT DO MOST PEOPLE NOT KNOW ABOUT HIM?

Before checking into a hotel, David likes to check out the rooms. If he doesn't like the layout or the view, he'll ask to see another.

Photograph by Danny Williams

David Reaume Construction & Design, Inc.
David Reaume
161 E. California Blvd.
Pasadena, CA 91105
626.795.7810
Fax: 626.793.1687
www.reaumeconstruction.com

roche**bobois**

France has given the world many things: Famed painter Claude Monet, celebrated chef Jean-Georges Vongerichten, and home furnishings giant Roche-Bobois. Recognized the world over for European Contemporary design, the 45-year-old company has 300 showrooms in nearly 30 countries, including four in Southern California (Los Angeles, Costa Mesa, and two in La Jolla), all owned and operated by Agnes Chouchan, the daughter of one of the Parisian founders of the company. Laurent Pingault is general manager at the L.A. store, where, in addition to a diverse range of furniture, clients have access to Pingault's substantial interior design talents, a service that reaches beyond the Roche-Bobois concept. Shunning ready-made concepts and design tricks, the designers always take a fresh approach, tailoring each project to the customer's taste and lifestyle. "We try to constantly reinvent ourselves," Pingault says, "and offer creative and extremely personalized solutions to our clients' needs."

Without preset ideas and with the goal of matching the personality of the customer, Pingault says, Roche-Bobois can redecorate a room from wall coverings and drapes to flooring and lighting in any style, whether strictly contemporary, Old-World traditional, or somewhere in between. The principal designer on all of the company's projects, he says, "I enjoy beautiful design in all its diversity of styles. I like to work on true contemporary projects as well as mixed environments in which a contrasted style can be used as a counterpoint."

Roche-Bobois
8850 Beverly Boulevard
Los Angeles, CA 90048
310.274.6520
www.roche-bobois.com

ernie**roth**

Each morning, Ernie Roth gets up early. Starting work before sunrise is a way of life after nearly 30 years as a production designer in the Los Angeles film industry. His talents were developed in classical training at California College of The Arts and through years of working in the varied fields of film production, interior design, and architecture.

Using sophisticated computer technology, Ernie presents his clients with photo-realistic views and walk-through movies, which enable the clients to visualize his design and collaborate with him, at the conceptual phase of the project.

"After many years of designing for the camera's point of view, I approach design thru the use of depth of space and form, a controlled use of light, and combinations of color and textures to both create the mood and control the eye of the viewer, as well as reflect my clients expression of self," he says.

My goal as a designer is to expand upon my clients' visions, to create personalized design solutions that reflect the unique personas of the homeowners, the use of photo-realistic illustrations and walk-though movies expedite this process.

Roth Interiors Inc., a successful design firm, has clients up and down the California coast.

LEFT
Ernie Roth Living Room: an eclectic collection gathered from years of travel. Armoire is 18th century French.
Photograph by Peter Christiansen Valli

FACING PAGE & INSET
Illustration: E. Roth/G. Wilson, Baker furniture window for a tribute to Commanders' Palace, New Orleans.
Photograph by Mark Berndt

TOP RIGHT
Ernie Roth bedroom. Furniture is French by Jacques Grange. Mirror is 18th century French gilt on wood.
Photograph by Mark Berndt

BOTTOM RIGHT
Rick and Cheryl Hoper master bath, Malibu, CA.
Photograph by Mark Berndt

Q&A
more about ernie

WHAT ONE PHILOSOPHY HAS HE STUCK TO THROUGH THE YEARS THAT STILL WORKS TODAY?

"I believe that good design not only enriches a space but also stimulates the user," Ernie says. "Good design does not depend on the size of a space but rather how that space is handled so that it appears inviting and creates a sense of well-being."

MEDIA RECOGNITION:

Ernie was the winning interior designer on *Designers' Challenge*, a popular show on HGTV. Ernie's transformation of a Malibu residence was seen by millions around the country.

Roth Interiors Inc.
Ernie Roth, Allied Member ASID
5966 San Vicente Boulevard, Suite 2
Los Angeles, CA 90019
213.590.1397
www.ernieroth.com

darrell**schmitt**

DARRELL SCHMITT DESIGN ASSOCIATES, INC.

Boutique hotels from Beverly Hills to Palm Beach to Cyprus. Golf clubs on the California coast. Resorts for Four Seasons Hotels in California and Hawaii. Spas in the Napa Valley and Indonesia. Ski resorts, beach side condos, homes from Houston to Aspen to Saudi Arabia and Japan, and even a few yachts. In his 33-year career, there is little in the world of high-end interior design that Darrell Schmitt hasn't done.

With each new assignment, the 15-person firm of Darrell Schmitt Design Associates takes a fresh approach in order to provide clients with imaginative solutions reflecting the highest standards of quality in design and execution. While observing trends in interior design fashion, Darrell often turns away from fads, instead concentrating on the evolution of architecture when searching for an appropriate design expression. "We are well-versed in historic design influences but create contemporary solutions that reinterpret the past for current needs," Darrell says. "We are renowned for interpreting our clients' desires into workable and elegant interiors which become classics in their own right."

Now with an international reputation, the designer grew up in the Midwest, where he manifested an interest in art and design early on. After studying architecture for two years at Kansas State University, Darrell channeled his energies and education toward interior design, completing his formal training at the Chicago Academy of Fine Arts, with additional study in France, Italy, and at the Banff Centre for the Arts in Alberta, Canada. After college, Schmitt moved south, to settle in New Orleans, Louisiana, in 1972. Within two years he opened both an art gallery and the first incarnation of his business, which handled a wide range of commercial and residential projects.

After 13 years at the helm of his own design studio, Schmitt relocated to Los Angeles, to join mentor James Northcutt and James Northcutt Associates, where he guided the firm to international stature before reopening Darrell Schmitt Design Associates in 1997.

In the years since his move to L.A., Darrell's work has received numerous awards and has been showcased in *Architectural Digest, Town & Country, Travel & Leisure*, and *Conde Nast Traveler,* among others. But accolades and recognition aren't the firm's motivation. "Above all, we value our clients' comfort," Darrell says. "We accept projects that present challenges and allow us to devise artistic solutions of notable integrity. And we take on only as much work as our core staff can handle through their personal attention. We place our emphasis on quality of design, service, and the development of long-term client relationships."

TOP LEFT
Suite living room at Calistoga Ranch, Napa Valley, CA.
Photograph by Tim Street-Porter

BOTTOM LEFT
Dining room of a private residence.
Photograph by Tim Street-Porter

FACING PAGE
Luxury suite at the Anassa Hotel, Polis, Cyprus.
Photograph by Henri del Olmo

Q&A
more about darrell

WHAT DOES HE THINK IS THE BEST PART OF BEING AN INTERIOR DESIGNER?

Darrell says that the most rewarding thing about his work is enhancing the lives of people by improving their living environments. To make someone's life better by making their home more beautiful is the biggest compliment, he says.

WHAT PERSONAL INDULGENCE DOES HE SPEND THE MOST MONEY ON?

A voracious reader, the designer loves to buy books.

WHAT DOES DARRELL LIKE MOST ABOUT DOING BUSINESS IN SOUTHERN CALIFORNIA?

The area presents a unique opportunity to create design that responds to the extraordinary sunlight.

Darrell Schmitt Design Associates, Inc.
Darrell Schmitt, ASID, CID
6030 Wilshire Boulevard
Suite 200
Los Angeles, CA 90036
323.951.9283

annewait

AW DESIGN, INC.

Anne Wait has a fail-proof approach to residential interior design: always keeping her clients' wishes in mind. "I don't inhabit a room," she says, "my client does. Therefore, I listen to what my client's needs and desires are. In a dynamic design all of the elements work together to create a space that is not only beautiful but also comfortable and inviting for the homeowner." Good communication and trust between designer and client are key to fashioning an environment that reflects her clients' tastes and lifestyles, Anne says.

Anne completed her design training in the UCLA Environmental Arts program and launched her firm, AW Design, Inc., in Los Angeles 25 years ago. An Atlanta native, she has the charm of a Southerner and a penchant for design that is timeless. "I think you should be able to design a room and in five years still think it looks terrific," she says. That doesn't mean, however, that Anne's work is restricted to one style. She can work in easy-going chenille one day and sophisticated silk the next. "I'm comfortable working with a variety of design styles," she says. "And I like to combine different design elements."

A member of the American Society of Interior Designers, Anne recently served as president of the Los Angeles chapter. In more than two decades in business, Anne has received numerous Presidential Citations from the chapter, as well as an ASID National Medalist Award in 2004. Her involvement with the organization has allowed her to pursue a variety of community service projects, including

LEFT
An understated room which combines silks, velvets, and rich wool fabrics in a monochromatic scheme, is highlighted by a mixture of art styles to create a warm and inviting space.
Photograph by Martin Fine

renovation and restoration of the mayoral suite at City Hall, as well as volunteer work with County USC Hospital, the Department of Children's Services at USC, Venice Family Clinic, and the Jenesse Foundation.

Anne was recently honored when she was chosen to design a 95-foot-long hallway for the Beverly Hills Garden & Design Showcase at Historic Greystone Estate. Her work has also been featured in the Pasadena Showcase House of Design, on HGTV's *Designers' Challenge,* and in *Fine Furnishings International, Global Architecture Houses, Kitchen & Bath Design News, Designing with Tile and Stone,* and *Audio Visual Interiors.*

ABOVE LEFT
Cherry paneling, a coffered ceiling, and walls that are faux painted using accents of copper metallic paint add interest to this family's pool room.
Photograph by Martin Fine

ABOVE RIGHT
Terra-cotta pavers accented with colorful ceramic tile inserts, a custom butcher block top, handmade tile backsplash, and beams that were salvaged from an old barn are combined with commercial stainless appliances to create an inviting kitchen.
Photograph by Martin Fine

FACING PAGE
A sophisticated dining room with a custom round table to accommodate eight people, elegant draperies with woven woods to filter the sunlight, and a custom rug with fabric border create a classic look to this room.
Photograph by Martin Fine

Q&A

more about anne

WHAT DOES SHE LIKE MOST ABOUT DOING BUSINESS IN SOUTHERN CALIFORNIA?

There are a number of things that make working in the area especially appealing, Anne says. To start, people lead a more informal lifestyle than in some other places in the country. Also, no specific style is prevalent in the region, which allows her to be versatile and follow a unique approach with each design. And Anne especially enjoys the resources — local manufacturers, abundance of imports, and new product introductions — readily available to designers on the West Coast.

WHAT PERSONAL INDULGENCE DOES ANNE SPEND THE MOST MONEY ON?

Anne loves to travel for both business and pleasure. She visits her friends and family across the country and takes a couple of ski trips and one international trip per year. In addition to working in L.A., the designer has worked on jobs in Hawaii, Park City, and Lake Tahoe.

AW Design, Inc.
Anne Wait, ASID
16801 Bollinger Drive
Pacific Palisades, CA 90272
310.454.1602
www.annewait.com

rozalynnwoods

ROZALYNN WOODS DESIGN STUDIO

For interior designer Rozalynn Woods, each new project is a chance to reinvent history. Every job is an exciting opportunity to conceive an original space while drawing on and reinterpreting the past. Thusly, the 20-year design veteran creates classic, uncluttered environments with a current point of view.

Rozalynn believes that the first step to good design is knowing where things came from. "Once you know what is regarded as the benchmark for good design," she says, "you can extrapolate and adapt it for your own work. I work hard to be fresh and innovative yet timeless," she says. For example, if a client loves the Empire style, Rozalynn might use that as a basis for her design then mix in contemporary, Asian-influenced pieces in order to bring the look up to date.

Rozalynn is a woman who is constantly evolving, continually redefining her perspective through a voracious curiosity that drives her to discover new things. In both her personal and professional lives she strives to be authentic. That means choosing organic foods when they are available and avoiding clothing that's not well-made from natural fibers. It also means that whenever possible she designs with an inventive eye using original art and furniture, always seeking the crème de la crème.

"My work is high style, no question," Rozalynn says, adding that she takes a very studied approach toward every component of interior design and makes a concerted effort to know what is best in every genre. "It has little to do with money," she explains, "and much to do with style."

And though she takes her work very seriously, striving always to create spaces that not only please her clients but are also worthy of her field, that doesn't mean her work is stuffy or without a sense of humor.

"Adding a fanciful touch to a room filled with very fine things adds another dimension," she says, giving as an example her mentor, whose home is filled with fine art, antiques, and high-quality upholstery. "She positions a small ceramic frog on the edge of a table. It's dangling legs and funny smile provide a lightheartedness that brings it all home," Rozalynn says.

And for the past two decades, home for Rozalynn has been in Los Angeles. The city offers an appealing diversity, from the people to the architecture, the avid traveler says. "One day you can be working on a '60's ranch house and the next you can be at a Wallace Neff estate."

ABOVE
Window treatments are sail inspired and filter light while softening the architecture of the room.
Photograph by Peter Christiansen Valli

FACING PAGE
Max Alto Simplice chairs flank a custom fireplace surround made of teak slatting, backlit by zenon lights. Low profile glass doors hide away clutter.
Photograph by Peter Christiansen Valli

ABOVE
The artwork is by local artist and part-time Parisian resident John Lincoln. A pair of 1940s black lac-
quered armchairs are from an Old Hollywood Estate.
Photograph by Peter Christiansen Valli

FACING PAGE
Vintage Richard Schultz patio table is paired with a sleek flexy mesh curve chaise from Henry Hall. The
Silent Gliss panels softens the hardscape of the concrete.
Photograph by Peter Christiansen Valli

Q&A

more about rozalynn

IF SHE COULD ELIMINATE ONE DESIGN STYLE FROM THE WORLD, WHAT WOULD THAT BE?

Rozalynn abhors bad reproduction furniture. "It adds nothing to a space, and in 40 years it will still lack the integrity missing when it was made."

WHAT SINGLE THING WOULD SHE DO TO BRING A DULL HOUSE TO LIFE?

Rozalynn likes high-gloss paint, whether on the ceiling or the walls or both, to wake things up.

WHAT IS THE HIGHEST COMPLIMENT SHE'S RECEIVED PROFESSIONALLY?

After her work was recently showcased in *Metropolitan Home*, a famous designer, whose work she has studied and admired for years, wrote to her, complimenting her on the featured project. Other publications that have featured her designs include *California Home & Design*, *California Homes*, and *Metropolitan Home*, on the cover.

Rozalynn Woods Design Studio
Rozalynn Woods
526 La Loma Road
Pasadena, CA 91105
626.441.1022

jean**zinner**

JAZ DESIGNS

While studying interior design at UCLA, Jean Zinner was required to design and build a kite — but to pass the course the kite had to fly! An interesting assignment to be sure, but only after starting her own firm did Jean fully appreciate the metaphor. She quickly realized that for her business to take off, her ideas, more than just being creative, had to fly with her clients. 23 years and thousands of rooms have proven that her ideas do fly. Jean's boundless energy, integrity, imagination, and creativity have translated into a thriving business and relationships that have spanned years and spawned multiple projects and many referrals.

A native Angelino with a background in fashion, photography, and horticulture, Jean has a natural ability for creating environments that work well for her clients' tastes and lifestyles. Though her personal favorite style is Spanish Colonial, Jean's portfolio is as diverse as her clientele. European Traditional, American Classical, California Contemporary, and more are all represented in her body of work. An award-winning designer, she especially enjoys helping clients discover their style preferences. Starting with a two-hour consultation, Jean guides them carefully through the process of building their dream, educating them on

ABOVE
The tumbled marble floor and rich Inca gold and terra cotta colorations of Cuzzo with a Malibu Potteries designed fountain are custom colorized to complement the Malibu tile risers.
Photograph by Martin Fine

LEFT
A reproduction of an authentic Malibu Potteries table forms the focal point of the living room. The Adamson House inspired wall stenciling, and 19th Century iron Mexican sconces completes the room.
Photograph by Martin Fine

TOP LEFT
An eclectic French/English room with canopy bed as the focal point. The ladder back chair, English spoon foot table and chest support the eclectic and feminine feeling of the period.
Photograph by Mary Nichols

BOTTOM LEFT
Knotty alder cabinets with a natural stain, Jerusalem limestone counters, cobalt blue tile backsplash, stainless steal appliances and an American cherry floor complete this kitchen.
Photograph by Martin Fine

FACING PAGE TOP
Chocolate oak distressed plank top table and console surrounded by six hand-carved walnut upholstered chairs. The chandelier is an iron and crystal Louis IV style.
Photograph by Martin Fine

FACING PAGE BOTTOM
A breakfast banquette, rattan sofa and ottoman provide cozy seating. Woven woods on the windows with the rattan add rich layers of texture to the monochromatic theme.
Photograph by Martin Fine

scale, color, texture, and furniture selection, then interpreting their desires with flair and skill.

For Jean, membership in the American Society of Interior Designers means more than a few letters after her name. She's served on her chapter's board and she's a past chairperson for both the Student Affairs and Education Committee and the Nominating Committee. For her outstanding support of interior design education, Jean received the Dorothy Peterson Award, one of the most prestigious A.S.I.D. honors.

Recently, Jean's work has appeared in the *Palisadian Post*, the *Los Angeles Times*, and *Los Angeles Home & Decor* magazine.

Q&A
more about jean

WHAT COLOR BEST DESCRIBES JEAN AND WHY?

Light blues and teal suit her best. "When I wear or work with these colors I always feel carefree, joyful, and happy," Jean says.

WHAT DOES SHE LIKE BEST ABOUT BEING AN INTERIOR DESIGNER?

The favorite part of her job is creating beautiful and unique environments that delight her clients.

WHAT DOES SHE LIKE MOST ABOUT DOING BUSINESS IN THE L.A. AREA?

Jean especially likes the diversity of architecture within the Los Angeles area, easy access to a myriad of design resources, and superior craftsmanship provided by the LA subcontractors.

JAZ Designs
Jean Zinner, ASID, CID
2202 Hill Street
Santa Monica, CA 90405
310.450.2056
www.jazdesigns1.com

DESIGNER: Linda Applewhite, Linda Applewhite & Associates, *Page 143*

NORTHERN CALIFORNIA

AN EXCLUSIVE SHOWCASE OF NORTHERN CALIFORNIA'S FINEST DESIGNERS

williamanderson

More than a preference for a certain style, William Anderson has a love for exceptional quality from all time periods, and the designer feels strongly about providing his clients with the very best in terms of both design and materials. For example, he says, exceptional fabrics can mean the difference in a good project and a great one. The goal, always, is to leave the client with a spectacular finished product that doesn't look "decorated" but, instead, relays a warm, personal feeling.

The firm specializes in fine furnishings and floor coverings for dining rooms, living areas, and master suites; it also does remodeling and space planning and has solid expertise with kitchens and baths. The most successful projects are those in which the client is fully dedicated to the process and engaged in the designer-client relationship, he says, recalling two very different jobs on the same street: one, a Norman Tudor; the other, a 1970's Moderne; both with extraordinary results due to the commitment and involvement of the homeowners.

William's 17-year-old company is a small one, which means clients have the luxury of plenty of face time with the designer himself. William does all of the consulting, shopping, and design, forever remaining true to the architecture of the space in which he is working and bringing to every job a background in fine arts, a knowledge of antiques, and a passion for color. Working with people and helping them realize their dreams through interior design is, for William, the greatest reward for his work.

LEFT
This 1912 Albert Farr living room was begun with the Lee Jofa toile 19th century chairs are in Old World weavers tapestry.
Photograph by David Duncan Livingston

ABOVE LEFT
Most pieces in this 1970's updated living room are Holly Hunt with console from Gulassa & Co.
Photograph by David Duncan Livingston

ABOVE RIGHT
A. Rudin leather chairs are paired with a wenge custom dining room table from Ocampo.
Photograph by David Duncan Livingston

RIGHT
Master bath was created from a closet. The sunken tub and sink are cast concrete, wall and floor are travertine.
Photograph by David Duncan Livingston

Q&A more about william

WHAT PERSONAL INDULGENCE DOES HE SPEND THE MOST MONEY ON?

A former museum director in his home state of South Dakota, William likes to invest in paintings. He also collects sterling silver, particularly pieces from noted California silversmith Allan Adler.

MOST PEOPLE DON'T KNOW THAT…

William substitutes on occasion as a church organist.

WHAT COLOR BEST DESCRIBES WILLIAM AND WHY?

"Orange appeals to me hugely," he says, "because it's a happy, warm color. I don't get to use it much, but is it fun when I do." His own home features lots of orange.

WHAT BOOK IS HE READING RIGHT NOW?

In Cold Blood by Truman Capote.

William Anderson Interiors
William Anderson
Allied Member ASID, CCIDC
2525 11th Avenue
Oakland, CA 94606
510.534.2502

lindaapplewhite
LINDA APPLEWHITE & ASSOCIATES

A home is the physical expression of the people who live in it, and its impact on their lives should not be underestimated," says Linda Applewhite, who for 20 years has given residents in the San Francisco Bay area beautiful, functional interiors.

Personal and nurturing environments are the goal of the Marin County-based firm, but Linda's approach is more comprehensive than style and the placement of objects. Her strengths include her use of color, juxtaposition, and whimsy. Additionally, she says, "I like to design rooms with very interesting architectural details that break the rules — rooms that surprise yet are classic." In addition to residential projects in California and across the country, Linda has been extensively involved in the design of the Mill Valley Inn, in Mill Valley California, the remodel and design of the Hotel Sausalito in Sausalito, California, and, most recently, the remodel and design of The Cottages of Napa Valley in Napa California.

Always team-oriented, Linda collaborates first with her clients and then with project architects, landscape designers, and contractors. In doing so, she creates homes in which interior and exterior spaces reflect and enhance each other. "Our mission is to help clients fulfill their personal design and space goals and express themselves in the selection of design elements while respecting the architecture and project site," Linda says.

In 2005, the designer, whom *California Home & Design* magazine has recognized as changing the face of design, began teaching the principles of design to others, showing them how to execute the essentials of design and find the inspiration and confidence to decorate their own homes. To this end, she has written a book on embellishing architecture, which will be published by Gibbs Smith in 2007.

ABOVE
Warm plaster walls, old sandblasted beams and antique brick floors give character to this California
Wine Country living room.
Photograph by Claudio Santini

FACING PAGE
Applewhite selected antique French pavers in golds and apricots for the island and backsplash of this
Wine Country kitchen.
Photograph by Claudio Santini

Q&A

more about linda

ON WHAT PERSONAL INDULGENCE DOES LINDA SPEND THE MOST MONEY ON?

She loves plants and flowers. Her home and garden are filled with an abundance of both.

WHAT COLOR DOES LINDA SAY BEST DESCRIBES HER?

Color is a pivotal element of Linda's designs. She believes that color has vibration and is necessary for an environment that feeds the heart and soul. Orange — the color of the sun — is the hue most suited for the designer's friendly, happy outlook on life.

AWARDS AND RECOGNITION:

Linda's design projects have been featured in numerous U.S. publications, including *House Beautiful, Elle, Bon Appetit, Travel & Leisure, Traditional Home, Women's Day, Sunset, California Home & Design, The San Francisco Chronicle,* and *The Los Angeles Times.* Her work has been published internationally in the Italian design magazines *Gioia Casa, La Mia Casa, Bravacasa, Bagno e Accessori,* and *House & Garden Thailand.* On television, viewers have discovered her design projects featured on HGTV's *Sensible Chic* and *Curb Appeal,* and on Food TV's *Ultimate Kitchens.*

Linda Applewhite & Associates
Linda Applewhite
510 Turney Street
Sausalito, CA 94965
415.331.2040
www.lindaapplewhite.com

geoffreydesousa

DE SOUSA HUGHES

Some people are fascinated by celebrities. Others have preoccupations that range from math to travel to certain kinds of food. Geoffrey De Sousa's obsession lies in design. The 43-year-old Boston native is completely wrapped up in what is not only his profession but also his passion: "It's the books I read. It's the movies I see. It's what I buy, where I go, who I am," he says.

Geoffrey is half of De Sousa Hughes, an interior design studio and showroom he owns and operates with Erik Hughes. The pair purchased the business in 1999, after many years of managing the business for its previous owner, interior designer Agnes Bourne. As joint creative directors of De Sousa Hughes, they have tripled the size of the showroom in the last seven years, creating a company that specializes in boutique lines that represent premier craftsmanship. The firm showcases more than 65 manufacturers of furniture, textiles, lighting, art, and accessories hand-selected from around the world. Geoffrey says, "the focus is on designs that can't be found elsewhere in the marketplace. Many of them from small, young, California-based companies, and all chosen for their hand and quality and commitment to a modern aesthetic."

Though De Sousa Hughes sells only to the trade, anyone is welcome to come in and browse, for the showroom is not just a resource for professional interior designers, it's a source of inspiration and education. "Ours doesn't feel like a multi-line showroom," Geoffrey says. That's because he's taken

LEFT
The warm walnut walls were the inspiration for the living room in this stately San Francisco 1920's Tudor. Custom upholstery made in England by George Smith.
Photograph by Cesar Rubio

ABOVE
De Sousa Hughes Showroom, San Francisco Design Center, circle squared coffee table by Geoffrey De Sousa; upholstery by George Smith; carpet by Rosemary Hallgarten.
Photograph by Cesar Rubio

RIGHT
De Sousa Hughes Showroom; Photographs by Rick Chapman; cairn shelf by Troscan Furniture; accessories from Chista.
Photograph by Cesar Rubio

FACING PAGE LEFT
Sea Cliff residence; custom sofa upholstered in Holland & Sherry fabric; custom headboard and screen upholstered in Joseph Noble; lamps by Leslie Anton.
Photograph by David Duncan Livingston

FACING PAGE RIGHT
Sea Cliff residence, 1920's lab table converted into a console from Swallowtail, SF. Glass Apothecary Jars & Shell Bowl, Urban Chateau, SF.
Photograph by David Duncan Livingston

great care to create room vignettes so that people can see how various lines work together and how materials can be used in unexpected ways. One might find an upholstered sofa from Ted Boerner coupled with a pair of club chairs from De Sousa Hughes's own line, accented with hand-thrown lamps by Lesley Anton and pulled together with a wonderful handmade Rosemary Hallgarten rug, for example.

As a nationally known interior designer for hire, Geoffrey takes only a few clients each year. In order to remain hands-on and form intimate relationships with his clients, he concentrates on just three or four large-scale projects, like the ongoing restoration of a 1920s Italian villa atop Russian Hill, complete with a domed living room ceiling adorned with a plaster relief of the zodiac. And then, of course, there are his own projects: constructing a modern house in Clarendon Heights and remodeling a Palm Springs retreat built in 1959 — proving that even when it comes to a vacation escape, he will pursue his life's work with fervor.

Q&A
more about geoffrey

WHO HAS HAD THE GREATEST INFLUENCE ON HIS CAREER?

"My parents," Geoffrey says. While some kids weren't permitted to hang a favorite poster in their bedrooms, Geoffrey's let him and his siblings express their individuality in their personal spaces. "My parents were always fixing things up. They transformed a 19th-century railroad barn into a wonderful space to house both of their businesses and took on the challenge of renovating a very neglected property that we all still consider home today. We were allowed to do what we wanted to do in our own rooms, and my mom encouraged us to be creative. At age 13, I had orange wall-to-wall carpet; a wonderful 1970s chocolate brown-lacquer bedroom set; orange, brown, and white wallcovering; and chrome photographer lamps — to say the least it was quite the departure from my parent's Massachusetts colonial.

WHAT'S ONE THING MOST PEOPLE DON'T KNOW ABOUT HIM?

Before moving to San Francisco 11 years ago, Geoffrey was an interior designer for Bloomingdale's. "I think my retail background provided the hands-on experience that has helped me to continue to provide our clients with the customer service they deserve and homes that speak of them," he says.

WHAT'S THE GREATEST COMPLIMENT HE'S RECEIVED PROFESSIONALLY?

Not long ago, one of his clients was quoted in a magazine, explaining that she liked working with Geoffrey because he is not a dictatorial designer. Instead of vetoing her ideas, he gently pointed her toward things she liked even better.

De Sousa Hughes
Geoffrey De Sousa
2 Henry Adams Street, Suite 220
San Francisco, CA 94103
415.626.6883
www.desoughsahughes.com

ABOVE
1920's San Francisco Tudor, Edwardian chair and ottoman by George Smith. Photograph by Michael Wolf; floor lamp by Michael McEwen; 1950's folding side table, JF Chen, LA.
Photograph by Cesar Rubio

FACING PAGE TOP
Presidio Heights residence, B&W art, Robert Longo. Carpet, Christopher Farr. Book table, Ted Boerner. Rope library table, Christian Astuguevielle
Photograph by Vittorio Visuals

FACING PAGE BOTTOM
Presidio Heights residence, dining table, Christian Liagre. Candelabra, Christian Astuguevielle.
Photograph by Vittorio Visuals

davidharris
& richardkasten

HARRIS & KASTEN, INC.

LEFT
A Swedish Neoclassical style bedroom furnished with early 19th century antiques, framed by silk drapery and hand stenciling. The period chandelier was found in Paris.
Photograph by Russell Abraham

RIGHT
Harris & Kasten murals create vistas of scenes along the Nile around this inviting dining room set with Buccellati silver, Fabergé China and antique Baccarat crystal.
Photograph by Russell Abraham

By the time David Harris and Richard Kasten came together to form their architectural and interior design firm in the early 1990s, both were established talents in their own right. Harris's reputation as an abstract expressionist artist and representational muralist had earned him such diverse clients as Caesar's Palace in Las Vegas and Chartered Bank of London in Northern California. Kasten had relocated to the San Francisco Bay area in 1981 and took the lead in designing the interior architecture for such projects as Birk's Restaurant in Santa Clara and the Los Altos Public Library expansion. Then the pair met at a dinner party in 1992.

Before long they were collaborating, with Kasten commissioning Harris's works for his commercial projects. After completing an office building together in Silicon

Valley they were asked to remodel a century-old home for a couple who saw their work. With complementary talents and an obvious synergy, joining their skills seemed like a natural step, and that first project provided a springboard for the artist and the architect to do what they'd already been thinking about: forming a partnership combining the traditional skills of a design firm with the fine art abilities of both men.

Today the two operate out of their Half Moon Bay home, where they have harmoniously merged their styles and tastes. Often, they are hired to work on a house from the ground up, in which case as he plans the house, Kasten strives to create opportunities for special works of art. Too, Kasten is responsible for the sensitive restoration, expansion, or updating of estate properties and apartment

residences. In addition to his architectural skills, Kasten joined Harris in painting. They rarely outsource work on their projects, preferring instead to do everything from faux finishes to ceiling murals themselves.

From the first conversation with these eccentric talents, it's obvious that Harris and Kasten are no ordinary designers — and their clients are no ordinary folk. Sought for their artistic bent, Harris and Kasten like to leave a bit of themselves in every project. They do that most often through elaborate wall and ceiling murals that drive their concepts for the rooms that they design. "When a room is totally designed it tells

a story," Harris says. "Sometimes it's a story about the client, sometimes it's a total fantasy. Either way, it takes you beyond the four walls."

ABOVE LEFT
A former carriage entrance becomes an outdoor salon, framed by all-weather draperies. David and Richard hand painted the Bamboo Trellis Mural overhead.
Photograph by Russell Abraham

ABOVE RIGHT
This spacious Tuscan-inspired kitchen replaces former cramped kitchen and pantry spaces and features a lofty vaulted ceiling. The center table rests on antique marble Griffins.
Photograph by John Canham

FACING PAGE
A Classic French Salon blends Asian and European Antiques. Display niches are silk-lined. David Harris' "Flower Fields, Normandy" hangs over the Louis XV console.
Photograph by Russell Abraham

jerryhettinger

J. HETTINGER INTERIORS

LEFT
Old World charm and elegance is one of the many styles a great design team can offer you. The most important part of that team is a qualified designer that can lead them.
Photograph by Douglas Johnson

RIGHT
A gourmet kitchen that is chic and yet functional.
Photograph by Douglas Johnson

Twenty-five years ago, Jerry Hettinger had a dream: to own and operate one of Northern California's leading interior design firms. To that end, he rented a 1,000-square foot space in Danville and set up shop. And as the community grew, so did J. Hettinger Interiors.

Today, Jerry owns his sprawling 13,000-square-foot office and showroom (and the shopping plaza where it's located), and his firm had gone from three people to employing 25, including 15 experienced designers.

The firm's work is concentrated in the San Francisco Bay Area, including projects in some of the finest homes in Danville, Alamo, Pleasanton, Livermore, San Ramon, Walnut Creek, San Jose and beyond, but J. Hettinger Interiors has taken on jobs as

far as Africa. With an average of 200 projects — both residential and commercial — on the books at a time, "We offer a complete range of interior design services," Jerry says. "This means we handle jobs large and small, doing everything from selecting a single piece of furniture to creating a total environment from conception on. Often we work with a client and the architect from the point of construction plans, detailing lighting, fireplaces, moldings, and built-ins, selecting marbles, tiles, and fixtures, and moving on to color palettes and furnishings."

The large-scale success of J. Hettinger Interiors is something that amazes even its namesake designer, and Jerry boils it down to a single objective: excellence. Such a lofty goal is accomplished with exceptional designers who focus on integrating

their clients' needs into the environments they create, superb teamwork from everyone involved on their many projects, and a commitment to bringing out the best in the spaces they work in.

Plus, Jerry says, "Customer satisfaction is our number one concern. Of course, we stand behind everything we sell. But we don't stop there. The confidence we have in our design service allows us to offer an in-home guarantee even on most special-order furnishings. We feel our clients deserve nothing less."

To mark 25 years of quality workmanship of gorgeous and interesting design, J. Hettinger Interiors recently released its first-ever signature furniture collection. "It's a combination of our talented designers'

minds at work," Jerry says. "To appeal to everyone, we've designed three individualized styles: contemporary, transitional, and traditional. A particular look is transformed by blending the textures, colors, fabrics, and shapes. Each stylized piece complements the others, creating a desirable, comfortable, functional, and inventive form. Frequently we custom-design furniture for our clients," he says. "Creating our own collection allowed our designers to be more creative and have more input."

With such a vibrant past, what does the future hold for the firm? Jerry won't speculate, preferring instead to let life — and business — take him where it may. One thing, however, that he will attest to is that dreams can come true.

Q&A
more about jerry

WHAT PHILOSOPHY HAS J. HETTINGER INTERIORS STUCK TO FOR YEARS?

When designing an environment, the firm's designers focus on the client's taste, lifestyle, and budget. When hiring people, Jerry concentrates not only on finding top talent but also on the character and personality of each candidate.

WHAT SEPARATES THE FIRM FROM ITS COMPETITION?

J. Hettinger employs a large ensemble of talented designers, a large showroom loaded with quality merchandise, an extensive inventory housed locally in two warehouses, competitive prices, and a guarantee of satisfaction. These distinguishing factors are what have propelled the company through two decades of success.

ANY AWARDS OR SPECIAL RECOGNITION YOU WOULD LIKE MENTIONED?

The firm has received a vast array of accolades in its 25 years in business. Its work has been featured in *Architectural Digest, Home & Garden, Northern California Home & Design, Diablo Magazine,* and *Design for Living.*

J. Hettinger Interiors
Jerry Hettinger
J. Hettinger Plaza
200 Hartz Avenue
Danville, CA 94526
925.820.9336
www.jhettinger.com

ABOVE
Symmetry and a dramatic focal point, creates a stunning guest room in monochromatic tone and unique textures.
Photograph by Douglas Johnson

FACING PAGE LEFT
A mix of texturally disparate elements and a piece of custom commissioned artwork set the tone for this casual, eclectic dining room.
Photograph by Douglas Johnson

FACING PAGE RIGHT
Classic geometric forms, curves and grids create a space that feels both comfortable and stimulating.
Photograph by Douglas Johnson

catherinemacfee

CATHERINE MACFEE INTERIOR DESIGN, INC.

Since 1989, Catherine Macfee has established a reputation for creating sophisticated interiors that are luxurious but livable. Her classic interiors feature an evocative blend of antiques, custom furnishings and artistic accessories that come to life in layers of texture and color. "I like a home to unfold, to have an ongoing sense of discovery for the owner," says Macfee. "My goal is to create interiors that spark people's curiosity and don't reveal themselves in one setting."

As principal designer of her eponymous firm, Catherine leads every project and manages a talented team of ten. A strong, intuitive designer with a background in fashion as well as interior design, Macfee enjoys getting to know her clients, learning what inspires them and then transforming that knowledge into interiors that enhance their lifestyles. Her projects range from urban pied a terres in San Francisco to grand and gracious vacation homes in Tahoe.

Aficionados of Macfee's style also head to her 4,000-square-foot store, Catherine Macfee Home, in the classic East Bay town of Orinda. The showroom, open to the public and to the trade, features Macfee's new custom, upholstered collection, as well as her hand-picked selection of antiques and one-of-a-kind accessories. A second store in Tahoe will open soon.

Signified by rich colors, luxurious textures and distinctive warmth, Catherine Macfee's projects have twice been honored by the ASID with its Western Interior Design Award of Excellence. Her work has also been featured in *San Francisco* magazine, *Sunset, California Home & Design, Tahoe Quarterly*, and many other publications.

ABOVE
Voted Mountain Home Kitchen of the Year, 2002.
Warm wood and copper hues highlight the commissioned hand-forged pot rack light fixture with mica and branch detail.
Photograph by David Duncan Livingston

RIGHT
Grand in scale yet conveying the intimate in atmosphere, the dining room appoints the most gracious elements to the Mountain lifestyle. Christofle, Bacarrat, and Herrend table service. English antique antler candelabras, Upper East Side, New York.
Photograph by David Duncan Livingston

FACING PAGE
As *Mountain Living* magazine Home of the Year, the master bedroom is yet another masterful signature stroke. Catherine MacFee Home Collection Furnishings, log four poster bed, tramp art armoire. Original French painted wedding chest dated 1796.
Photograph by David Duncan Livingston

Q&A

more about catherine

HER FRIENDS WOULD SAY …

That she's driven and fearless. When she gets an idea in her head, she pursues it full speed.

WHAT ONE PHILOSOPHY HAS CATHERINE STUCK WITH FOR YEARS THAT STILL WORKS FOR HER TODAY?

"My goal," she says, "is to capture the attention and imagination of the people who enter a room. If my design does that, I have done my job."

WHAT SINGLE THING WOULD SHE DO TO PERK UP A DULL HOUSE?

Color is a hallmark of Catherine's designs, and she believes it is the simplest way to transform a room to bring it to life.

Catherine Macfee Interior Design, Inc.
Catherine Macfee, Allied Member ASID, NKBA
2 Theatre Square, Suite 122
Orinda, CA 94563
925.254.2600
Tahoe, CA 530.584.5200
www.macfeedesign.com

philip**meyer**

PHILIP J. MEYER LTD.

A leader in the interior design field, Philip Meyer has been creating gorgeous, interesting rooms for more than 25 years. He discovered his passion for design at the age of 20, while traveling with an architect friend through the United States, Mexico, and Central America.

Philip's contemporary education and extensive knowledge of antiques, gleaned from three years as international director of sales at a high-end antiques dealer, combine for a unique blend of advanced design based on classical and neoclassical standards, which Philip says give a space substance and familiarity. His projects are a varied mix of residential and commercial commissions — country clubs, medical suites, anything that requires a residential bent — in the San Francisco Bay Area, as well as Florida, Utah, Oregon, and various other resort locations. He might be working on the restoration of a 1920's Neogothic manse one day and a rustic mountain-top resort the next.

Drawing inspiration from the great American designers of the first half of the 20th century — Elsie de Wolf, Billy Baldwin, Francis Elkins — Philip approaches each new project entirely independently of past projects, working toward innovative design solutions that will withstand the test of time. For Philip, this means using architecture as the starting point, working with a neutral color palette, and layering old and new, soft and hard, textural and smooth, to satisfy the client's wants and needs and leave them with a graceful, personalized environment.

Philip J. Meyer Ltd.
Philip J. Meyer, ASID
1005 Bush Street
San Francisco, CA 94109
415.673.6984
www.philipjmeyerltd.com

suzannemyers

ELITE INTERIOR DESIGN

t's the day before Thanksgiving and Suzanne Myers rushes from room to room in a client's 15,000-square-foot home. The high-energy designer will have the draperies installed before the homeowner's corporate jet touches down (and holiday guests arrive). And she'll be at her own Norris Canyon Estates manse when she gets his call saying that her transformation of their home is beyond his family's wildest dreams and they're absolutely thrilled.

Do it right, or don't do it at all. It's the maxim by which Suzanne lives her life and operates her business, Elite Interior Design. She also believes in doing things herself, ensuring that the end result of her every endeavor is as close to perfection as can be.

Whether preparing herself for a trip to France or working on a client's French-style chateau, the tireless interior designer starts with intensive research and stops only after she's exhausted her considerable resources. "It doesn't cost anything to do your homework," she says. "I will explore anything and everything and take each idea to the nth degree." This approach has earned Suzanne the respect of her peers, the trust of her clients, and a coveted spot at the top of her field.

The Canadian-born designer has an effusive manner and a palpable enthusiasm for her job. In fact, she discovered her "mad passion" at a very early age. One of four children of

ABOVE
The living room is draped in Schumacher Italian linen moiré with Houlès French trim. Dessin Fournir
crackled lacquer and chinoiserie coffee table.
Photograph by Douglas Johnson

FACING PAGE
The kitchen has honed French limestone floors, dramatic dark cherry cabinetry with French pewter
hardware. Hand-painted Italian pottery and hood hand carved in stone with a grape motif.
Photograph by Douglas Johnson

affluent parents, Suzanne grew up traveling the world and living in homes filled with objects of impressive quality and beauty. Her childhood experiences instilled in her an appreciation for all things gorgeous and interesting and fostered worldly sensibilities with regard to interior design, architecture, and landscaping.

In her typical all-or-nothing style, she earned a bachelor's degree in fine arts in 1975 from the California College of Arts and Crafts, graduating with a 4.0 grade-point average. She then established a successful retail shop and design practice in San Francisco, which she ran with a partner for 15 years. In 1989, she opened her current firm, focusing on complete remodels, additions, new construction, and interior design.

A stickler for detail and follow-through, Suzanne doesn't delegate. Instead, she prefers to handle every aspect of every project herself. A higher level of client communication comes from confining her business to what she can take care of herself, she explains. By always being available to her clients and listening carefully, she is able to interpret their wishes in ways that far exceed their expectations.

Suzanne's work has been published nationally and internationally, most recently on the cover of *Sunset* magazine. She has appeared on HGTV's *Interiors by Design* and over the years has participated in eight San Francisco Decorator Showcase showhouses, winning numerous awards. But the greatest accolades, she says, come from clients who call her at home, overjoyed with the gift she has given them.

LEFT
Entry hall graced with Flemish tapestry and Pakistani area rug. Background in Venetian plaster, with antique glaze, stone arches and niches.
Photograph by Douglas Johnson

FACING PAGE LEFT
Antique Tonsu with Modigliani painting in stone niche with a rock crystal votive.
Photograph by Douglas Johnson

FACING PAGE RIGHT
Breakfast room includes "Ironies" table and chandelier, arm chairs are William Switzer with Nobilis fabric, and Greeff fabric on valances and Roman shades.
Photograph by Douglas Johnson

Q&A
more about suzanne

WHAT IS THE HIGHEST COMPLIMENT SHE HAS RECEIVED PROFESSIONALLY?

An interior designer whom she admires once told her that they had followed her career and aspired to have a business like hers.

WHAT SINGLE THING WOULD SUZANNE DO TO BRING A DULL HOUSE TO LIFE?

Suzanne finds that dramatic lighting brings magic to a space. In fact, her most unusual project involved lighting recessed in a beveled mirrored ceiling with jeweled medallion joints.

WHAT DO MOST PEOPLE NOT KNOW ABOUT HER?

She is a fantastic cook. Specializing in Italian and French dishes, she's famous for her seafood lasagna and coq au vin.

Elite Interior Design
Suzanne Myers
213 Lyndhurst Place
San Ramon, CA 94583
925.837.6688
www.sgmelitedesign.com

~173~

emily**taylor**

EMILY TAYLOR INTERIORS

Emily Taylor stumbled into interior design. And in doing so she tapped into a passion and talent within herself that she'd certainly seen glimpses of but hadn't realized to their potential.

After earning an art history degree from Skidmore College in New York, Emily spent a few years working in advertising before getting married and moving to Boston. Eight years ago, she relocated a second time, to California, where a friend asked Emily to help decorate her house. Her work was so well-received that she's had a steady stream of clients ever since.

Described by those close to her as the Martha Stewart of the West, Emily's strengths lie in her abilities to listen to her clients and design around their desires. It's not a matter of taste, the 39-year-old says. "A lot of people have great taste, but pulling it all together to make a cohesive, beautiful space can be difficult. That's the job of a designer," she says.

With an eye toward the superb styles of Nancy Lancaster and Frances Elkins, Emily strives for the same kind of longevity with interiors that re-create the layered effect often found in the homes of the wealthy and well-traveled. She starts with fine antiques, fabrics, and rugs, then she might add a Plexiglas table or hair-on-hide-covered stools for a contemporary edge, always keeping her finger on proper scale and balance, something for which her work in the 2005 Decorators' Show House in Atherton was recognized.

Previously, Emily was recognized for excellence in 2002 as the recipient of the California Home and Design Achievement Award. Additionally, her work has been published in *Gentry* magazine.

Emily Taylor Interiors
Emily Taylor
270 Bridge Road
Hillsborough, CA 94010
650.401.6563

suzannetucker

TUCKER & MARKS INTERIOR DESIGN & DECORATION

LEFT
Inspired by Coco Chanel's apartment, Suzanne dressed this room to the nines, hanging a pair of antique ornate gilt mirrors from Christie's on brown lacquered walls.
Photograph by Tim Street-Porter

RIGHT
A lesson in luxury: Suzanne covered the walls of this powder room in a satin fabric and matched the 19th-century French rock crystal sconces with rock crystal faucets.
Photograph by Ken Gutmaker

Suzanne Tucker's portfolio is a broad, deep body of work for some of the Bay Area's most well-heeled residents. Major art collectors, founders and chairmen of Fortune 500 companies, and others of acclaim have solicited the designer for her spectacular interiors marked by a skillful combination of antiques and contemporary pieces, tailored curtains and upholstery, a masterful blend of colors and textures, and appropriate architectural scale.

In business for herself since 1986 — when she opened her firm with husband and partner Timothy Marks — Suzanne began her career under the tutelage of the Father of California Design, the legendary Michael Taylor, after studying interior architecture at the University of Oregon and earning a bachelor's degree in design from UCLA. Some members of her award-winning team worked with Mark Hampton, David Easton, Barbara Barry, and other design greats before joining Tucker & Marks. Today, the 18-person company has a distinguished client list and a broad spectrum of projects throughout California, as well as on the East Coast and parts in between.

And that means that Suzanne has to be versatile. She might be working on a formal San Francisco residence or a Hawaiian retreat one day and planning the interiors of a villa in Sonoma or a sprawling ranch house in Montana the next. Regardless of style and location, her approach is consistent. "My goal is for clients to live comfortably with or without formality. It's all about a high level of interior design that is approachable," she says.

Suzanne's press list goes on for pages. In 2005 alone her work was featured in *Architectural Digest* (April and January), *California Home & Design*,

San Francisco magazine, the *San Francisco Chronicle*, *Fine Furnishings International*, and on the *Forbes* website. A Marin mansion she designed earned the cover of *Traditional Home*'s October 2004 issue. In May 2002, Sotheby's included her in its first-ever New York By Design sale of property from the collections of decorating icons of the 20th century. The following year she was named by *Robb Report* as the Best of the Best in the Interior Designers category.

And for all her well-deserved acclaim, the designer herself is exactly what she hopes her interiors are — approachable. Suzanne is not only a talented professional, she's also exceptionally nice, intelligent, and witty, which is why her clients are "lifers." She's either redone their homes again and again, or they've asked her to design their second and third residences.

ABOVE
Her clients wanted an old European look so Suzanne sourced a 17th-century Dutch lacquered table and had paneling and bookshelves made of aged English brown oak.
Photograph by Tim Street-Porter

FACING PAGE
A quiet opulence reigns in this living room, whose color palette was inspired by the tones in the antique Ushak rug and coromandel screen.
Photograph Tim Street-Porter

paul**wiseman**

THE WISEMAN GROUP

LEFT
The two-story library holds a collection of rare books and maps on exploration. The domed plaster ceiling is embellished with a star chart.
Photograph by Matthew Millman

RIGHT
This 18th century Portuguese colonial desk is juxtaposed with an 18th century Queen Anne chair and a 19th century bronze statue of a Samurai warrior.
Photograph by Matthew Millman

Paul Wiseman's mother, a high school home economics teacher, taught him to make a mean pear pie. The secret to a light, flaky crust, he says, is Crisco. And the secret to great interior design? "Appropriateness, appropriateness, appropriateness."

And as simple as that might sound, "You really have to analyze this," says the 30-year design veteran. "Is the style appropriate to the location? Is it right for the architecture? Does it fit with the philosophy and lifestyle of the person who's going to live with it? You can't do Hollywood glitz in a Tudor mansion or Malibu Beach in a French chateaux."

Named Designer of the Year in 2000 by the American Society of Interior Designers, Paul has appeared four times on *Architectural Digest*'s list of the top 100 designers, and in 1999 the Robb Report recognized him as one of the world's five top designers. Clearly, the man has talent. He's got an eye for quality and an innate ability to bring together the right colors, fabrics, furniture, and lighting in an extraordinary and elegant way. His interiors are breathtaking works of art, delightful spaces to covet and envy. But his success is not entirely about creativity, he says. It's also about integrity.

"Since day one, I have believed that a strong business sensibility … would differentiate us in the design industry," he says. "The way we do business is very professional." That's a tenant that all of The Wiseman Group's 30-plus employees ascribe to. It's also something his clients (the roster includes many big names) appreciate. "I have a lot of very happy clients."

However, Paul never takes the business of interior design too seriously. Though he brings superlative attention to detail and exemplary design services to every project, whether country estate, private jet, or exclusive golf club, he also recognizes the big picture: "We're not saving lives; we're just decorating," he says. "Have fun!"

A vibrant, personable demeanor is one thing that helps the native Californian — who has the tan to prove it — continue to enjoy his work. A good sense of humor is another, as is finding time for himsel. Though his business has flourished for three decades, Paul stays connected to his spiritual side through regular meditation. And when he needs a creative boost, he heads to the garden to pull weeds. "There, I re-center myself, and the juices start coming again."

TOP LEFT
This living room of a 1930's Gardner Daily home uses antique and custom-made furnishings and an antique Ushak carpet.
Photograph by Tim Street-Porter

BOTTOM LEFT
The oval living room of a 1920's San Francisco apartment contains antique furniture and artwork, a Samarkand carpet, Fortuny ottoman and a Michael Taylor sofa.
Photograph by Tim Street-Porter

FACING PAGE LEFT
The living room in a Maybeck inspired home combines pre-Columbian figures, an 18th century Buddha, and two of Andy Warhol's 1973 Mao Tse-tung silk screens.
Photograph by Christopher Irion

FACING PAGE RIGHT
In this dining room from a 1930's home, The Wiseman Group preserved the overdoors and shell niches and added an English pedestal table.
Photograph by Christopher Irion

Q&A

more about paul

WHAT PERSONAL INDULGENCE DOES HE SPEND THE MOST MONEY ON?

Paul began traveling at age 17, when he set out for a three-month tour of Europe after graduating from high school. Since then, his extensive world travels have taken him to the farthest parts of the globe. Bhutan, Peru, and South Africa are among his favorite locales.

WHAT COLOR BEST DESCRIBES PAUL AND WHY?

Black is the hue with which he most closely identifies, "because it's the combination of all color," he says. Similarly, Paul's design style encompasses all genres. "It's completely diversified — from traditional to contemporary to tropical."

WHO HAS HAD THE MOST INFLUENCE ON HIS CAREER?

Through the years, Paul has continuously been inspired by the work of designer Renzo Mongiardino — specifically, his level of detail and his historical referencing. "He took things to such a high level," Paul says. "The closer you look, the more you see."

The Wiseman Group
Paul Vincent Wiseman, ASID
301 Pennsylvania Avenue
San Francisco, CA 94107
415.282.2880
www.wisemangroup.com

DESIGNER: Randy Boyd, Thurston/Boyd Interior Design, *Page 187*

SOUTH COAST

AN EXCLUSIVE SHOWCASE OF SOUTH COAST'S FINEST DESIGNERS

randy**boyd**
THURSTON/BOYD INTERIOR DESIGN

W hen Randy Boyd completes a project, he wants to leave having clearly reflected his clients' personalities. One of Randy's primary goals is to give his clients' homes a "collected" look that exudes a strong sense of styling along with a welcome and comfortable energy.

Randy has been an interior designer for 26 years. His traditional sensibilities combine styles and time periods. For example, he might design a home with predominantly European antiques but will then incorporate touches of Asian artifacts to add interest or whimsy. "We are never static with what we bring to the mix," Randy says of his 20-year-old firm, noting that he prefers heirlooms to trendy pieces.

His repeat clients — and there are many — have come to depend on Thurston/Boyd for every aspect of their homes' design. The full-service firm has a strong background in construction and lends its expertise to all areas of the building process. "I am very involved with the architect, contractor, subcontractors, and the landscape artist," Randy says. "That way, everyone works together, culminating in a project that flows smoothly and is completed in a timely manner."

In addition to offering interior design services, Thurston/Boyd also operates a lovely retail boutique in Laguna Beach. The shop carries a carefully edited selection of hand-blocked fabrics; antiques from France, Spain, Italy, and Colonial Mexico; and various art forms by local artists.

LEFT
A French Normandy farmhouse designed as a client's mountain retreat. The use of yellow and cranberry fabrics helped to create a warm and inviting great room along with rustic French antiques.
Photograph by Aidin Mariscal

ABOVE LEFT
A feeling of warmth and comfort in this oceanfront living room is brought together with tall bookcases, antiques, artwork and inviting upholstery.
Photograph by Aidin Mariscal

ABOVE RIGHT
Warm walls and soft colors — along with antiques — bring charm to this guest bedroom.
Photograph by Aidin Mariscal

RIGHT
Shades of blue and red along with antiques, blue and white porcelain and chinoiserie accents complement this English cottage living room.
Photograph by Aidin Mariscal

FACING PAGE
A grand living room is made more intimate by designing the space with several conversation areas. The designer selected fabrics in shades of green, terracotta and camel to complement the plaster walls and antique terracotta floors.
Photograph by Aidin Mariscal

ABOVE LEFT
A large family kitchen, the cabinets are finished in a warm distressed stain, while the center island is done in an antiqued painted finish. Counters are an antiqued marble.
Photograph by Aidin Mariscal

ABOVE RIGHT
A sense of calm is achieved by the use of warm soft colors in shades of cream and pale terracotta.
Photograph by Aidin Mariscal

FACING PAGE LEFT
This traditional dining room includes bookcases and a comfortable reading chair which looks out to an inviting English garden.
Photograph by Aidin Mariscal

FACING PAGE RIGHT
This loggia lends itself to entertaining. The space includes a sitting area with fireplace and dining area. The designer selected vintage wicker seating, iron accents and an antique dining table from Paris. The loggia enjoys views of the courtyard with antique fountain to one side and the formal pool and pavilion to the other.
Photograph by Aidin Mariscal

pia**chapman**

Known best for her modern, post-modern, and contemporary designs, Pia Chapman turns ordinary spaces into extraordinary places. A world-class professional with an impressive portfolio and an equally noteworthy roster of clients, the designer creates interiors that are, at once, arresting and understated.

German born and raised, Pia drove her mother crazy rearranging the furniture from the time she could move a chair. She moved to California in 1987 and, after attending Design Institute of San Diego, worked first for a furniture company and then at the city's largest architectural firm before striking out on her own with Cocoon Studio.

Today, her full-service company handles projects large and small, always going the extra mile, attending every detail, and delivering design that is "100 percent right." That means that all of the client's wants and needs have been considered and met with the best possible solution, right down to the last door handle or fabric choice.

Growing up in Europe and traveling extensively from a very young age helped to shape Pia's approach to art and interiors and gave her an unusual view of the world. Equally important, however, are her daily interactions with clients, contractors, suppliers, and others, whether friends, clients, or colleagues.

A woman of cutting-edge style and substance (and the mother of triplets), Pia says that people are the greatest influence in her designs and in her life. "If you really open your eyes and your mind, they teach you so much."

LEFT
Back To The Future: A 21st century interpretation of a 1950's diner featuring professional grade appliances. The kitchen is designed with generous use of industrial stainless steel, concrete countertops and custom walnut cabinets.
Photograph by David Harrison, Harrison Photographic

Q&A

more about pia

WHAT IS ONE THING PEOPLE DON'T KNOW ABOUT THE DESIGNER?

She loves animals. Had Pia not become an interior designer she says she would likely have chosen a career caring for them. With two rescue dogs of her own, she belongs to several animal activist groups.

WHAT DOES SHE ENJOY MOST ABOUT HER WORK?

"Creating something that pleases my clients," Pia says. "If they are happy, I am happy." The designer views every job as a chance to give her clients what they want — and then some.

Cocoon Studio
Pia Chapman, ASID
1110 Torrey Pines Road, Suite I
La Jolla, CA 92037
858.551.2511
www.cocoonstudio.com

ginaharris

DESIGNS BY GINA MARIE

Gina Harris recently returned from France and Italy on a buying trip. "We picked up some wonderful pieces and accessories for one of my Newport Coast clients. We also took some fabulous photos of local Paris and Tuscany, which I will paint in my art studio." Gina's paintings show in several galleries nationwide. "I set no limits on myself in art and design. I work in all genres and styles, helping each client design a unique space," she says.

"My gift is bringing all elements together to create pleasure and comfort in my clients' homes." Gina is gifted in interpreting a person's style, combining textures, colors, fabric, furniture, and art in a harmonious way that expresses each client's personality. "This is their work of art, and I'm helping them create it. I always listen to my clients' dreams and what they're imagining for themselves. Everything they talk about becomes important in the design. Every home is an individual expression."

With a diverse portfolio — from beachy Ralph Lauren to an opulent European feel or stark modern where art is the only focal point — Gina does it all. "I believe that life is art, and we express this in our homes," she says. "We all want to live in an environment that restores our spirits and I help make that happen."

ABOVE
Comfort and elegance are found in this inviting living room with the hand tufted sofa and original Tuscan scene, that Gina Marie painted from a recent trip to Italy, along with accessories found in France.
Photograph by Marc Tarlton/Tarlton Studios

LEFT
A French farmhouse table made with reclaimed church wood sits under a custom distressed ceiling with a flickering candle light fixture to create an intimate yet festive mood in this dining wine room.
Photograph by Marc Tarlton/Tarlton Studios

Designs by Gina Marie
Gina Marie Harris
Laguna Beach, CA
949.275.2321
designsbyginamarie@yahoo.com

sheldonharte

HARTE BROWNLEE & ASSOCIATES INTERIOR DESIGN

Sheldon Harte quickly lists the names of the interior designers who have most influenced his career: John Cottrell, Michael Taylor, Thomas Pheasant, Victoria Hagan, Elsie DeWolf, and Billie Haines. "They all do really interesting work," he says. And like those he looks to for inspiration, Sheldon also makes a mark with the rooms he creates for his clients. Long before he knew the names of design icons, however, Sheldon's career path was being shaped by his parents: His mother was a connoisseur of fashion design, and his father was a landscape designer. And though as a child he didn't necessarily appreciate being dragged along on his mother's antiquing trips, those outings were preparing him for his future.

The Southern California native established his small company 21 years ago and is known today as one of the area's foremost interior design firms. Well-versed in the building process and all styles of architecture, Sheldon has worked in nearly every possible style, from contemporary to country, always giving his clients stylish, comfortable homes — or as he puts it: "beautiful yet approachable" spaces.

Approachable is a term that the designer hopes can also be used to describe his persona. An imposing six-foot-one, with the air of confidence you might expect from a man with his accomplished portfolio, Sheldon brings to his work a sense of humor and a glass-half-full attitude. His job, he says, is not only to create wonderful, meaningful environments for his clients, but also to make the process fun for them. A designer with a keen intuition and trust in his own instincts, Sheldon does this, in part, by making swift decisions and sticking to them, thus keeping his projects on track in terms of both time and budget. The very best projects, he says, are those in which the clients defer to his advice and give him the freedom to apply his expertise to interpret their tastes.

Sheldon has appeared on various HGTV segments. His work has been published in *Traditional Home, California Home, Window & Walls, Coast Magazine*, and others.

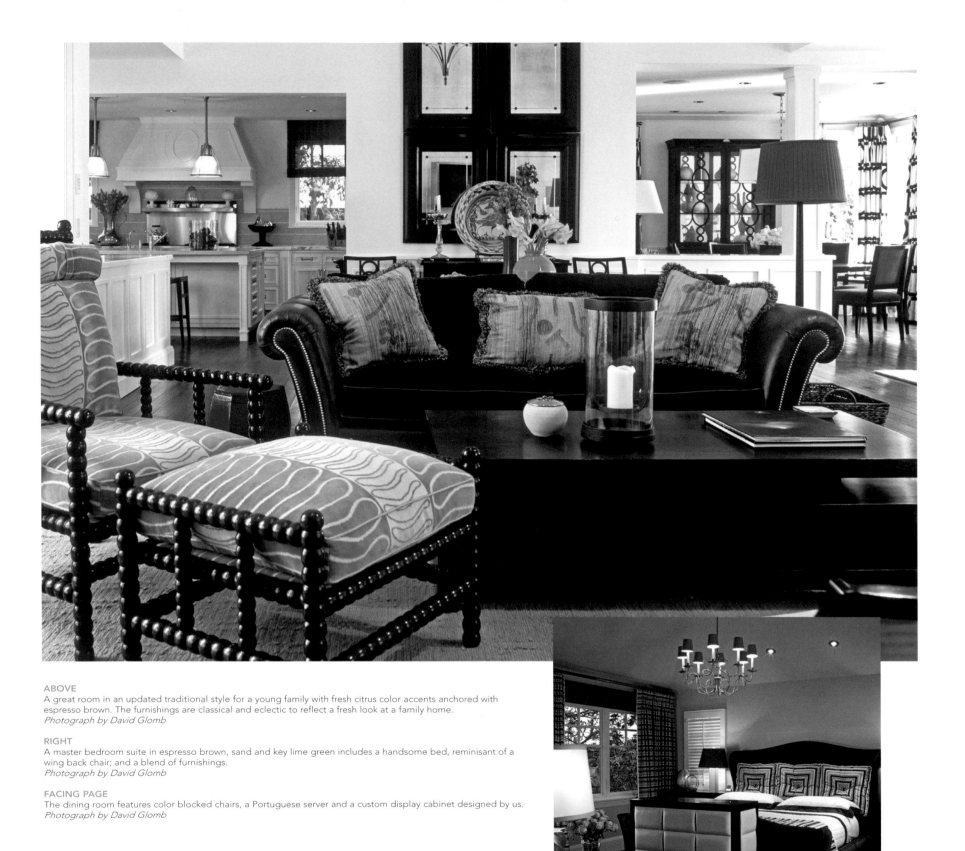

ABOVE
A great room in an updated traditional style for a young family with fresh citrus color accents anchored with espresso brown. The furnishings are classical and eclectic to reflect a fresh look at a family home.
Photograph by David Glomb

RIGHT
A master bedroom suite in espresso brown, sand and key lime green includes a handsome bed, reminisant of a wing back chair; and a blend of furnishings.
Photograph by David Glomb

FACING PAGE
The dining room features color blocked chairs, a Portuguese server and a custom display cabinet designed by us.
Photograph by David Glomb

sheryll|jackman

SEASIDE HOME

Southern California's Coastal Lifestyle emphasizes open floor plans, outdoor living, and homes oriented to capitalize on views. Living spaces need to combine subtle and elegant detailing, blending indoors and out, to create a single, harmonious unit. Sheryll Jackman believes in companioning understated elegance with upscale refinement while incorporating surrounding natural beauty.

One only needs to step into Seaside Home, Sheryll's retail ateliers, to know instantly what "coastal lifestyle" is all about. Located in the heart of two historic seaside villages, Seaside Home is a reflection of Sheryll's exceptional credentials as an interior designer and of Southern California's special style of seaside leisure and grand traditions. Truly unique and eclectic, the ateliers showcase Sheryll's expertise in all things relating to a comfortable living environment. With more than 25 years of experience in the design and development of custom homes,

specialty boutiques, restaurants and hotels, she brings together all of the elements that represent her unique experience and philosophy.

At Seaside Home, an enviable selection of furnishings and accessories, combined in lifestyle settings, are presented in an inviting and comfortable way. A kitchen, used as the cash wrap, is not only a display for the firm's expertise in kitchen design, but it also conveys the sense of actually being in someone's home. Serving soft drinks, wine, and coffee to the store's clients while they make their selections is easily accommodated.

Sheryll has brought together many of the world's most renowned and sought-after lines and presented them in a fresh and inspirational way. Baker Furniture, Seaside Home's signature line; along with McGuire; Oscar de la Renta; Janus et Cie; Century Furniture; Hancock and Moore; and Hickory Chair are representative of

the manufacturers shown. Exclusive European bedding lines, including Sferra, Yves Delorme, and Matouk, are displayed abundantly alongside many elegant bath and shower products. In addition, William Yeoward Crystal, Lynn Chase, Jay Strongwater, Arte Italica, Mariposa, and many other complementary lines round out the tabletop offerings. Asha carpets and Merida sisals are among flooring options. Interior design services, of course, are always available.

Sheryll is President and Director of Design for The Jackman Group, a Coronado-based multidisciplinary firm offering residential planning, design, and construction. In addition to being a professional member of the American Society of Interior Designers, she is a licensed general contractor as well as a real estate broker for Jackman Realty.

ABOVE
Seaside Home, La Jolla, is an exquisite two-story Design Atelier, representing the world's finest
home furnishings and accessories, enchanting gifts, lavish interior design services and unsurpassed
quality and elegance.
Photograph by Greg West

FACING PAGE & INSET
Coastal lifestyle Defined: this space is the epitome of Southern California living.
(Outside View) Continued from the first page, this elegant outdoor living area demonstrates Sheryll
Jackman's seamless transition from indoor to outdoor living design. Located on Coronado Island,
Sheryll Jackman designed the living area with a fireplace and outdoor seating — sprinkling in bits
of coastal décor.
(Inside View) Elegant detailing in the furniture and fabric provide understated elegance and
upscale refinement, while the entire floor plan is open, focusing on bringing the outside into
the home. The outdoor living space beautifully maintains all of the elegance of the interior while
focusing on the dramatic views of the San Diego skyline.
Photographs by Greg West

Seaside Home
Sheryll A. Jackman, ASID, CID
Coronado Island
1053 B Avenue
Coronado, CA 92118
619.435.8232
www.seasidehomecoronado.com

La Jolla Village
7509 Girard Avenue
La Jolla, CA 92037
858.454.0866
www.seasidehomelajolla.com

mary**kellejian**
POLO BAY INTERIORS

Mary Kellejian's clients are never far from her mind. On vacation, out with friends, or shopping for herself, the certified interior designer is constantly thinking of design and keeping an eye out for unusual pieces to surprise and delight her clients and incorporate into their interiors. Even while sleeping she is working on design solutions: Ideas often present themselves to Mary in her dreams, forcing her to scramble out of bed and jot down notes or sketch out a concept.

Her 20-year-old firm, Polo Bay Interiors (named for its proximity to both polo fields and the Pacific Ocean) is a full-service company with a staff that includes Mary's daughter, Kelli, who is also a theater and television set decorator. With complementary styles and perspectives both youthful and experienced, Polo Bay skillfully tackles a wide range of work — from managing projects from the ground-up to redecorating a single room — with professional savvy and a consistent goal: creating functional, attractive living spaces.

A seasoned, hard-working designer with a reputation for bending over backward for her clients, Mary describes her personal style as classic, distinguished by fine, timeless fabrics and furniture. With a firm understanding of her strengths, she interprets clients' styles with inspiration and ingenuity, forgoing trends and delivering interiors that withstand the test of time.

Polo Bay Interiors
Mary Kellejian, ASID, CID
3790 Via De La Valle
Del Mar, CA 92014
Palm Desert, CA 92260
858.259.1334

kristina**koerper**

SAN JUAN KITCHENS & HOME

LEFT
This elegant kitchen boasts a farm sink, new radius window, cherry cabinetry, limestone countertops, Italian tile backsplash, antique gold faucet, and porcelain handles. The linen drapes are finished in European trim.
Photograph by Gail Owens

RIGHT
This kitchen features handmade clay floor tiles, cherry hand-finished cabinetry, copper and brass accessories, and Italian tile back splash. Antique terracotta bricks create chimney stack.
Photograph by Gail Owens

Kristina Koerper opened San Juan Kitchens & Home on Swallows Day 2004 in historic San Juan Capistrano, California. Located there, Kristi has the opportunity to design and remodel homes that range in style from grand, European elegance to contemporary loft apartments to quaint beach cottages.

Soft-spoken and intuitive, Kristi begins each of her projects by meeting her clients in the environment she'll be working in. Then she deftly executes a vision that is true to the homeowners, their home, and its surroundings. The new design can be a complete home remodel, from floor up, or new home construction. From the hardscape to the finishing details of draperies and furniture, Kristi's work is a soulful endeavor. "This is their private space, my desire is that what we create, enhances the lives that live here," Kristi says.

Kristi looks forward to developing her own line of custom furniture, fabrics, bedding, lighting, and other surprises in the near future.

San Juan Kitchens & Home
Kristina S. Koerper
31815 Camino Capistrano, Suite #13
San Juan Capistrano, CA 92675
949.481.7743
www.sanjuankitchens.com

regina**kurtz**

ALPHA DESIGN GROUP

After 25 years, interior design has become second nature to Regina Kurtz. Working with a two-pronged philosophy built on Louis B. Sullivan's doctrine, "form follows function" and Mies van der Rohe's "less is more," the award-winning entrepreneur finds that the ideas for and implementation of elegant spaces flow easily. Her experience has given her the confidence and the know-how to assess a client's needs and then deliver an environment that is at once striking and comfortable.

Always a creative type, Regina studied fashion design at the Fashion Institute of Technology and worked in New York City's fashion industry. She turned to interior design after her children were born, eventually returning to school and earning a degree in art and interior design from San Diego State University. "I have my children to thank for my career," Regina says, referring to the fact that when she decorated their rooms friends were awestruck. "That's when the light bulb went off," she remembers.

Regina also has her husband and business partner, Al Isenberg, to thank for her business. Al runs the operations side of Alpha Design Group, allowing his wife to focus her talents on the creative aspects of the business. Whether working on multimillion-dollar mansions or spatially challenged high-rise condos, Regina exhibits a broad range of style, from formal traditional to casual contemporary. As a result, she is known throughout San Diego for her practical, livable, and inviting spaces.

A client-centric designer, Regina takes pride in the fact that she is not recognized for a signature look, saying, "The day someone can walk into a home and say, 'Regina Kurtz designed this' is the day that I have failed my client. Knowing that I make a difference in my clients' everyday lives is, for me, the best part of the job."

Q&A
more about regina

WHAT IS THE HIGHEST COMPLIMENT SHE HAS RECEIVED PROFESSIONALLY?

When one of her colleagues asked her to consult on the remodel of their home.

WHAT ONE ELEMENT OF STYLE OR PHILOSOPHY HAS REGINA STUCK WITH FOR YEARS THAT STILL WORKS FOR HER TODAY?

FUNCTION is the foundation on which she builds all of here designs.

WHAT DOES SHE LIKE MOST ABOUT DOING BUSINESS IN SOUTHERN CALIFORNIA?

"Because we are not steeped in tradition the way that the East Coast is, there are more opportunities to think outside the box," she says. "Creativity is welcomed."

Alpha Design Group
Regina Kurtz, ASID, CID
1747 Hancock Street, Suite B
San Diego, CA 92101
619.295.8110

kristin
lomauro-boom

KRISTIN LOMAURO INTERIOR DESIGN

LEFT & RIGHT
In the beach side guest suite, the classic antiques share the room with the modern
art work by "Jamali." The upholstered headboard in Kathryn Irelands, Ikat stripe,
sets the tone that is carried into the guest bath.
Photographs by Edward Gohlich Photography, Inc.

Kristin Lomauro-Boom showed the first signs of her career path as soon as she was strong enough to move a chair, rearranging her bedroom every time her mother turned around. At age 10, when her grandparents began looking for a new home, she helped out by drawing the furniture layouts on the floor plan. It was shortly after she went to her first Kips Bay Decorator Showhouse, in New York City, where she was mesmerized by the work of the famed John Saladino. And if she didn't know before, she knew then: She was destined to be an interior designer.

After graduating with a B.A. in Interior Design from Marymount University in Arlington, Virginia, Kristin began working for several well-known designers in

Los Angeles and Manhattan. Kristin then started her design firm eight years ago in New York, eventually moving to San Diego with her husband. Her design approach is to be current without being trendy, sticking to designs with classic appeal and letting the distinct architectural details serve as the guiding force in each project. She strives for a balance between vintage and new, sleek lines and those that have an organic flavor or texture. Thusly, she enjoys the challenge to be able to marry styles that might at first seem in opposition.

Another design philosophy Kristin follows is the importance of good lighting. Interesting lighting gives a room dimension, she says, and it's the perfect way to bring a dull room to life. Adding wall sconces and chandeliers to a room can

ABOVE
Red rouses the library of a Georgian style home, traditional club chairs sit upon a Tibetan rug from
Aga John Oriental Rugs, Los Angeles.
Photograph by Edward Gohlich Photography, Inc.

RIGHT
A guilded mirror reflects the red-accented bookshelves.
Photograph by Edward Gohlich Photography, Inc.

FACING PAGE
An antique mahogany roll top desk tucks perfectly next to the library bookshelves
for writing.
Photograph by Edward Gohlich Photography, Inc.

compensate for a lack of architectural detail. They can fill a space and create a focal point. Like a great pair of designer shoes and belt can complete an outfit, good lighting can pull a whole room together, she says.

After the lights go out at KLID, Kristin switches gears and dedicates many hours each month to reaching out to the community. Her membership in the Junior League of San Diego helps her find a necessary equilibrium between meeting the wishes of her wealthy clients and serving the needs of those who are less fortunate, particularly the educational needs of underprivileged children. One of her largest efforts has been to help bring art back into the lower income schools of San Diego. The Art Cart program has reached 2,500 fourth graders with crafts, supplies and instruction. Another effort brought 5,000 reading books into one school.

Q&A
more about kristin

WHAT PERSONAL INDULGENCE DOES KRISTIN SPEND THE MOST MONEY ON?

Fine bed linens and letterpress stationery.

WHAT BOOK IS SHE READING RIGHT NOW?

Ask and It's Given, by Esther and Jerry Hicks

WHAT DOES SHE LIKE MOST ABOUT BEING AN INTERIOR DESIGNER?

Getting to know her clients on a personal level and their lifestyle, which in turn allows her to better understands their design needs.

Kristin Lomauro Interior Design
Kristin Lomauro-Boom, Allied Member ASID
3307 Fourth Avenue
San Diego, CA 92103
619.298.6607
www.kristinlomauro.com

wendyann**miller**

WAM INTERIOR DESIGN

Wendy Ann Miller calls herself a "serial designer," meaning she typically handles more than one project for her clients. It also means she barely has time to think as one project ends and another begins.

As a full-service firm that works all over the country, WAM Interior Design might work with a client from the home construction phase one year, redecorate the client's second home the next, and handle an addition to the first several years later. In fact, Wendy's still doing work for her very first clients 20 years after opening her design studio, which today comprises 3,000 square feet of the latest innovations in residential and commercial design — hard-surface materials like updated tile and stone offerings, the newest in hardware, and one of the most extensive fabric libraries in Southern California, which includes domestic and imported fabrics and trim. "People call me back because I give clients a space where they feel at home when they are at home," she says.

Though that might sound simple, it takes intuition, sensitivity, skill, and the ability to excise her own preferences. "If I did it for me, everything would look like the Palace at Versailles," she jokes. Of course, if you want over-the-top, one-of-a-kind frou-frou mirrors and gilt, the designer will see that you have it. But if sleek, spare, and ultra-modern is your style, Wendy can do that, too. "I've done both and everything in between," she says, "sometimes on the same day, in the same house."

Above all, Wendy says, no matter the genre, "The spaces we live in should be over-the-top beautiful. When you're at home, you should feel like you're someplace really special — a great restaurant, a luxurious hotel suite, a romantic retreat — that reflects your lifestyle. My job is to take a dream and make it reality."

LEFT
Design House 2003: Luxurious portal to relaxation for every woman who considers herself a queen. Embroidered silks, lavish chenilles, and miles of trim complete the journey.
Photograph by Martin King

Q&A

more about wendy ann

WHAT PERSONAL INDULGENCE DOES SHE SPEND THE MOST MONEY ON?

"Shoes and handbags," is a quick and easy answer for Wendy. Though she has more than her fair share of fancy heels from Manolo Blahnik, Rene Caovilla, and the like, she's known more for her tennis shoes. The designer goes everywhere in sparkly, silver-trimmed Sketchers' mules. "And when they get dirty, they go in the trash. I have about 30 backup pairs."

She doesn't, however, mind getting dirty in her garden. She loves flowers and has a beautifully landscaped yard. "Gardening is therapy for me," she says.

WHAT IS ONE OF THE MORE UNUSUAL PROJECTS SHE'S WORKED ON?

Wendy was hired to create an English pub underneath the Knudson mansion in Glendale, California. With a four-week timeline, the space had to be excavated and outfitted with everything, including a full-blown wine cellar, for the client's wife's 40th birthday. "We worked in 24-hour shifts," Wendy recalls. "I slept on the floor in a sleeping bag."

WAM Interior Design
Wendy Ann Miller, Allied Member ASID
1938 North Batavia Avenue, Suite C
Orange, CA 92865
714.283.0694
www.waminteriordesign.com

davidrance

DAVID RANCE INTERIORS

David Rance works on the concept that design is what surrounds the client, providing the setting for the client's life. "A client has an idea of what they like, but a designer has to have the ability to take them where they have not imagined," he says. "A designer should not be the person who gives clients what they want, they could do that themselves. A designer is a director of the imaginative creations, leading the way and directing the artisans to complete a vision that becomes the client's environment.

David Rance Interiors, located in the Artist Village in Santa Ana, was established in 1989. Working from a loft studio where the firm has been since 1992, David is inspired by the creative atmosphere of the area. The studio is surrounded by artists, architects, sculptors, and advertising companies. Sounds from the cascading water of a large water fountain carved from travertine by a local artisan filter through the firm's second-story windows, adding to the creative environment within. "We take inspiration from our daily lives and extraordinary events," David says.

New construction and major remodels provide a full spectrum for David's talents, which he applies to all aspects of each job's design. "We work on a project from dirt to the last spoon on the table," he says. Much of his work reflects a clean-lined style. "I'm not a person who is going to do frilly, overly cluttered design."

Designing for celebrities and even Saudi Arabian royalty, David enjoys getting to know his clients, developing relationships that continue for years after their projects are finished.

LEFT
Newport Beach: Classic, elegant and casual setting done with custom quality furnishings. This was created for the clients to relax and entertain.
Photograph by Scott Rothwall

He considers many of his Orange County clientele friends, having followed them from one stage of their lives into several others, as families grow, needs change, luxuries expand — always working with the clients' ways of life, entertaining and pursuing their dreams. "My design has to reflect the client's lifestyle, and it has to be refined and detailed with classic ideals," he says.

David is proud of his ability to make rooms multifunctional. Though most rooms have a primary space plan, today's clients want flexibility in their homes. David explains that there are different ways to stage a room, depending on the time and occasion. Recently he designed a contemporary-styled home with an adjustable dining room. "I provided two square dining tables for eight settings each. Then I created an abstract coffered ceiling with a

ABOVE LEFT
Corona Del Mar: Dining with sleek definition. This room allows multiple layouts for large and small dining possibilities. Contemporary sophistication with class.
Photograph by Scott Rothwall

ABOVE RIGHT
Corona Del Mar: With a flavor of Bali, and the color of many cultures, this kitchen came together. The sculpted archway, and the random tile add to the exotic flavor of this gathering space.
Photograph by David Johnson

FACING PAGE TOP
Newport Beach: Kitchen and intimate dining area. Use of the dark woods, stainless steel, and the stone mix together to create an inviting environment.
Photograph by Scott Rothwall

FACING PAGE BOTTOM
Pelican Crest: Glamorous Hollywood and 1920's Paris meet for the media room. The exotic woods, period pieces, and Lalique combine to create this lavish retreat.
Photograph by Scott Rothwall

monorail lighting system, so the client could move the lighting as the table configurations changed for different entertaining styles," he says.

David believes that a project should be awe-inspiring, no matter the size. Use of new items and fresh, innovative ideas develop into dynamic presentations. "I want every turn to be a new experience for people coming into my clients' homes."

Interior design has become a wonderful element to David's life. He truly enjoys his profession. This creates a very enjoyable design experience for David's clients. He is a believer in the saying "if a man loves what he does, he will never work a day in his life." Of course, there are challenges along the way, but the old adage is true for the talented designer. Because of that belief and because he enjoys his work, it shows in the creative selections and innovations provided to his clientele.

TOP LEFT
Corona Del Mar: Contemporary living, color and abstraction. This image captures the clean and art inspired essence of this residence. Architectural detail and lighting enhance the space.
Photograph by Scott Rothwall

BOTTOM LEFT
Corona Del Mar: Grand entertaining, with a killer ocean and light view that invites every guest to partake, is the point of this room. "Come on in and be part of this room."
Photograph by Scott Rothwall

FACING PAGE
Pelican Crest: This is true dining in elegant sophistication. The dining space can be totally enclosed with drapery. The adjacent wet bar in Art Deco details adds an adjacent repose to contemplate our lives.

David Rance Interiors
David Rance, ASID, CID
207 North Broadway, Suite A
Santa Ana, CA 92701
714.835.2408
www.davidrance.com

lena**brion**

LEFT
The wall at the head of the custom bed provides a focal point for the room and privacy to the
bathroom beyond.
Photograph by Carol Pierce

RIGHT
The back of the wall accommodates additional storage and an intimate setting for final
grooming touches.
Photograph by Carol Pierce

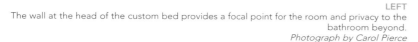

Lena Brion, president of the award-winning Brion Reilly, comes by her creative genius honestly. Growing up on Vancouver Island, Canada, Lena and her sister wore clothes their mother made by hand, and the floors of their home were covered by rugs woven on the family loom. Lena remembers being intrigued by a chair her older sister crafted from a grain container and the exquisite gift wrap she designed from newspaper. So for Lena, a career with a creative bent was a natural choice. "I cannot think of a time when I was not creating something or thinking about creating something," she says.

A graduate of Portland's Bassist College, now the Art Institute of Portland, Oregon, Lena relocated to California and entered the interior design field in 1987, focusing on high-end corporate interiors. She and her staff have earned a reputation for their classic contemporary interiors. In a single year, the firm won coveted ASID awards for excellence in three categories: residential, commercial, and health care.

Lena flourishes in the presence of variety and enjoys an ever-changing mix of projects. Though much of her work remains in the corporate realm, in the last decade, the 42-year-old designer has turned her eye more toward residential interiors. Reluctant at first, she has found it surprisingly satisfying, she says, because "it's closer to people's hearts."

Inspired by the European giants of modern design — Alvar Aalto, Le Corbusier, and the like — Lena's interiors are uniquely her own. She doesn't chase trends or model her designs on someone else's; she simply listens to her clients' expectations and lets her imagination guide her. And that's a formula that seems to please everyone, for despite having designed just a handful of kitchens, in 2005 the firm's design was chosen from among 70 entries as the Grand Prize Kitchen of the Year in the *San Diego Home/Garden Lifestyles* magazine competition.

ABOVE & RIGHT
The horizontal lines of the wood grain enhance the relaxed feeling of this sophisticated
kitchen. The close attention to detail keeps the cabinets looking simple.
Photographs by Hewitt/Garrison

FACING PAGE
Details and choice of materials make all the difference. The durability and warmth of this
material and the ease of care make this spot a popular hang out.
Photograph by Hewitt/Garrison

Q&A
more about lena

WHAT DOES SHE LIKE BEST ABOUT BEING AN INTERIOR DESIGNER?

"I find satisfaction in creatively finding solutions for improving flow or efficiencies in a space," she says. "And I like to bring a space together in such a way that it has personal meaning for the client."

WHAT COLOR BEST DESCRIBES HER?

The designer and mother of two has a great zest for life and says that green, the color of grass, leaves, and spring buds most resembles her. Plus, she says, green also inspires calm and security, something she strives to provide her clients and her own family.

WHAT ONE THING WOULD LENA DO TO GIVE LIFE TO A DULL HOUSE?

An expert in space planning, Lena would clean out the clutter and create focal points to revitalize a home.

Brion Reilly, Inc.
Lena Brion, ASID, CID
646 Valley Avenue, Suite A
Solana Beach, CA 92075
858.755.9011
www.brionreilly.com

pamela**stein**

STEIN/GRAY INTERIOR DESIGN

P amela Stein is strikingly modest. The soft-spoken interior designer often dresses in jeans and a tee, letting her clothing take a backseat to her natural beauty. Likewise, she doesn't much like to talk about herself, preferring instead to discuss the work for which she is passionate.

A Palm Desert native, Pamela began designing professionally 23 years ago, working first at a large firm and later joining with Nanette Lamoure-Gray to form Stein/Gray Interior Design in 1994. (Nanette recently retired, but Pamela continues the excellent work of the respected company.) Though Stein/Gray does serve private residential clients, Pamela primarily designs interiors for model homes, creating spaces that will capture the attention and imagination of potential homebuyers. Her achievements in this arena have earned her nominations for both MAME and Laurel awards — coveted prizes for new-home marketing and merchandising.

Starting with the goal of showcasing the architecture of a room and following the philosophy that details distinguish good design from great design, Pamela sets the stage for people fall in love with their environment. Her work in the model home industry has allowed her to develop a flair with most every style: "Contemporary, country cottage, Spanish hacienda — it's all over the board," she says. This flexibility with styles serves her private clients well. With a full range of possibilities, she hones in on their deepest desires and gives the homeowners design that flows from room to room as well as from the inside to the outside.

LEFT
Desert Villa. Coral and soft sage on an oyster palette brings the inside out. Offering a view of a most prestigious golf course, 12-foot ceiling, chenille drapery panels, Kentia Palms, orchids, and luxurious textiles. Timeless style, cool and inviting.

Q&A

more about pamela

WHAT PERSONAL INDULGENCE DOES SHE SPEND THE MOST MONEY ON?

The designer is very family-oriented and has a tight network of close friends. One of her favorite ways to spend time — and money — is sharing a nice dinner with the people she loves.

IF SHE COULD ELIMINATE ONE DESIGN/ARCHITECTURAL/BUILDING STYLE FROM THE WORLD, WHAT WOULD IT BE?

Patient and tolerant, Pamela can appreciate what she herself might not choose to live with. "I wouldn't take away anything from the world," she says. "Everything is valuable in its own way."

Stein/Gray Interior Design
Pamela Stein
29552 Spotted Bull Lane
San Juan Capistrano, CA 92675
949.347.0378

elizabeth
thiele**barkett**

ROSS THIELE & SON, LTD.

Founded in 1932, Ross Thiele & Son, Ltd. continues to operates, in many ways, with an old-fashioned, hands-on approach. John Thiele, at 85, is still active in the company his father started. John's daughter, Elizabeth Thiele Barkett, joined 19 years ago, making it a third-generation family business. The oldest design firm in the San Diego area, Ross Thiele & Son today runs a full-service design studio and antiques showroom in the heart of La Jolla.

As the firm's principal designer and a self-proclaimed workaholic, Elizabeth lives and breathes interior design, devoting 100 percent to making her clients feel special and giving them homes that reflect their lives, families, travels, and personalities. Before attending design school, she spent four years living in and traveling to foreign lands. That experience has proved invaluable in her career, providing inspiration for her designs and serving as common ground with her well-traveled clientele.

European and Continental antiques are a trademark of the firm's work, though they are not necessarily used in every project, Elizabeth says. Her work typically falls in the range of traditional/eclectic with a focus on Old World styles — Spanish Colonial Revival, French Country, and Tuscan. Services are tailored to meet the specific needs of each client and run the gamut from a complete interior package for new construction to assisting in the selection of fabric for reupholstry.

The work of Elizabeth and the company's other designers has been featured in numerous publications, including *Architectural Digest, Better Homes & Gardens, San Diego Home/Garden Lifestyles, South Coast Style*, and *Decor & Style Magazine*.

TOP LEFT
This spacious country French bedroom offers a fresh colorful
respite, with its upholstered bed, hand-painted striped walls, and
a comfortable reading area with natural light streaming in.
Photograph by Gail Owens

BOTTOM LEFT
This large, beamed ceiling family room in the heart of the house,
is a gathering place for multiple activities of all ages, with the
comfort of overstuffed sofas for casual conversation, while others
play at the game table or pool table.
Photograph by Gail Owens

FACING PAGE LEFT
Pale yellow walls with white mouldings, beautiful English
landscapes, parquet wood floors, collections of blue and
white porcelain draw you into this elegant living room of
Old World charm.
Photograph by Edward Gohlich Photography, Inc.

FACING PAGE RIGHT
This kitchen — with its crisp white cabinetry with white marble
tops and a blue granite island — is the cheerful workplace for
a talented chef. A hand-painted tile backsplash with fruits and
vegetables and large wood mantle over the cook top brings
pattern and color accents to the sunny space.
Photograph by Edward Gohlich Photography, Inc.

Q&A

more about elizabeth

WHAT PERSONAL INDULGENCE DOES SHE SPEND THE MOST MONEY ON?

"There's nothing better than a nice glass of wine and a fine dinner at the end of a long day," she says.

WHAT ONE THING WOULD SHE DO TO BRING A DULL HOUSE TO LIFE?

Adding color, art, and accessories are the fastest, easiest ways to make a room pop, she says.

WHAT COLOR BEST DESCRIBES HER AND WHY?

Though yellow appears often in the designer's work — "It's warm and cheerful but also a somewhat neutral background," she says — Red is the shade that she loves best. It's prominent in her wardrobe and her home.

WHAT MIGHT HER FRIENDS TELL YOU?

Elizabeth is a sensitive, open person. She's a loyal, true friend.

Ross Thiele & Son, Ltd.
Elizabeth Thiele Barkett, ASID, CCIDC
7425 Girard Avenue
La Jolla, CA 92037
858.454.2133
www.rossthiele.com

robert**wright**

BAST/WRIGHT INTERIORS

For Robert Wright, interior design doesn't stop at the end of a job or even the end of the workday. "I live it," he says. Not only does he create breathtaking design for his clients, but it's his number one personal indulgence as well.

Passionate about architecture and the "built environment" since college, Robert has worked as an interior designer for 28 years. He's been principal at Bast/Wright Interiors for 14 years. The eight-person firm handles both commercial and residential jobs, though Robert prefers the latter for the opportunities to get to know clients personally and to work with the area's finest contractors and tradesmen.

With senior designer Kellie McCormick, ASID, and a host of talented staff designers, the firm offers the collaborative synergy of a large company with the personal attention of a smaller one. Team members work together to come up with cutting-edge design solutions and stay abreast of one another's projects, so there's always someone on hand to provide immediate answers to clients with questions or concerns.

The firm's goal with every project is to seamlessly integrate interior design and architecture. One of Robert's design philosophies is to leave each space with enough "breathing room" so that it can evolve with his clients' changing lives. "I encourage my clients to be intimately involved in the design process and to personalize their space in a way that truly reflects who they are and what is important to them. That is what makes a house a home rather than an interior design installation," he says.

A leader in the interior design industry from the onset of his career, Robert has taught design at the university level for two decades. He's been an advocate and spokesperson on legislative and other issues that effect his profession. A consummate ASID volunteer for more than 20 years, he has served on the board of directors and was elected national ASID president for fiscal year 2006.

ABOVE LEFT
The 18th century Spanish dining table and the Persian Sultanabad rug are design focal points of the intimate dining room.
Photograph by Brady Architectural Photography

ABOVE RIGHT
The living room's coffered ceiling was designed using reclaimed aged beams and faux leather panels featuring classic Spanish decorative motifs.
Photograph by Brady Architectural Photography

RIGHT
A variety of textures in the living room furnishings and accessories add warmth and interest.
Photograph by Brady Architectural Photography

FACING PAGE
The view out the kitchen window is of California's Santa Margarita mountain range.
Photograph by Brady Architectural Photography

Q&A
more about robert

WHAT DOES HE LIKE MOST ABOUT BEING AN INTERIOR DESIGNER?

"I find it very rewarding to see the incredible impact that interior design has in providing a better quality of life for people where they live, work, and play," he says.

AWARDS AND RECOGNITION:

Robert is a widely published designer. His work is regularly featured in *San Diego Home/Garden Lifestyles* and San Diego magazines. He has received numerous awards, including several ASID San Diego Chapter Design Excellence Awards and the Ethel M. Siegelman Memorial Award for Outstanding Chapter Member. He considers his nomination and acceptance into ASID's College of Fellows his highest professional honor.

Bast/Wright Interiors
Robert Wright, FASID
1701 University Avenue
San Diego, CA 92103
619.299.5591
www.bast-wright.com

karen**ziccardi** & brooke**ziccardi**

ZICCARDI DESIGNS

The distinguished clientele of Ziccardi Designs get a double dose of talent. The mother-daughter team of Karen and Brooke Ziccardi provides clients with the experience that only three decades in the interior design business can bring as well as a fresh, youthful approach to creating gorgeous, interesting environments.

With a master's and a doctorate degree in environmental design from UCLA and a portfolio that spans the globe and includes the homes of entertainers, entrepreneurs, corporate CEOs, hoteliers, and royalty, Karen has finely honed her ability to transform the needs and wishes of her clients into a reality that surpasses expectations. A childhood spent at her mother's drafting table fostered Brooke's enthusiasm for interior design. She joined her mother's established practice five years ago, after earning a bachelor's degree in business from the University of Southern California and graduating from UCLA's interior design program.

Their boutique design firm specializes in all aspects of design and space planning with an emphasis on custom interior architectural detailing. First-hand research of authentic architecture allows Ziccardi Designs to gain a global view of trends old and new, which they then meld with classic styles. From a contemporary-style penthouse in Shanghai to a private Napa Valley winery estate to an oceanfront Italian-style manor, their work begins with an underlying foundation of line, form, color, texture, and spatial relations and is driven by an international vocabulary fueled by continual travel.

Karen and Brooke are dedicated not only to designing beautiful, functional interiors, but they also strive to build trusting relationships with their clients through a collaborative effort — ensuring a spectacular end result.

ABOVE
Rich fabrics, textures and furnishings combine to provide an intimate bedroom setting incorporating a cozy seating area, complete with fireplace and access to a large terrace overlooking the Pacific Ocean.
Photograph by Peter Christiansen Valli

FACING PAGE
Working closely with client, architect, contractor and landscape architect, Ziccardi Designs became part of the team that transformed the clients' vision of an authentic Tuscany inspired villa into reality.
Photograph by Peter Christiansen Valli

Q&A

more about karen & brooke

WHAT ONE ELEMENT OF STYLE OR PHILOSOPHY HAVE YOU STUCK WITH FOR YEARS THAT STILL WORKS FOR YOU TODAY?

Always work with the fundamentals of good design and dare to break the rules once in a while!

WHAT SINGLE THING WOULD KAREN & BROOKE DO TO BRING A DULL HOUSE TO LIFE?

"A party," Karen jokes,."For example, white walls might be considered "boring" by some, but actually can provide the client and develop design solutions to satisfy their requirements."

Ziccardi Designs
Karen Ziccardi
Brooke Ziccardi
3188 Airway Avenue, Suite D
Costa Mesa, CA 92626
714.556.8080

THE PUBLISHING TEAM

Panache Partners, L.L.C. is in the business of creating spectacular publications for discerning readers. The company's hard cover division specializes in the development and production of upscale coffee-table books showcasing world-class travel, interior design, custom home building and architecture, as well as a variety of other topics of interest. Supported by a strong senior management team, professional associate publishers, and a top-notch creative team of photographers, writers, and graphic designers, the company produces only the very best quality of these keepsake publications. Look for our complete portfolio of books at www.panache.com.

We are proud to introduce to you the Panache Partners team below that made this publication possible.

Brian G. Carabet

Brian is co-founder and owner of Panache Partners. With more than 20 years of experience in the publishing industry, he has designed and produced more than 100 magazines and books. He is passionate about high quality design and applies his skill in leading the creative assets of the company. "A spectacular home is one built for entertaining friends and family because without either it's just a house...a boat in the backyard helps too!"

John A. Shand

John is co-founder and owner of Panache Partners and applies his 25 years of sales and marketing experience in guiding the business development activities for the company. His passion toward the publishing business stems from the satisfaction derived from bringing ideas to reality. "My idea of a spectacular home includes an abundance of light, vibrant colors, state-of-the-art technology and beautiful views."

Wayne Howard

Wayne is the associate publisher in northern California for Panache Partners. A long-term resident of the San Francisco Bay Area, he has spent over twenty-five years in the publishing industry creating custom tourism and consumer magazines. "A Spectacular Home is one that is aesthetically exciting and yet immediately welcoming and comfortable."

Allison Hatfield

Allison Hatfield grew up in a big house in the woods in Alabama. She later lived in tiny apartments in Dallas and the surrounding communities, where she spent more time in an office than at home. She now resides in a brownstone neighborhood in Brooklyn, New York, where she can feel the rumble of the subway whenever it passes beneath her building. Allison's idea of a spectacular home is one that's filled with sunlight, love, and dogs. Hers currently has all three.

Peter Christiansen Valli

Peter Christiansen Valli is a nationally recognized architectural photographer whose work has been featured in numerous books and ad campaigns. His photographs have appeared in Architectural Digest and other shelter magazines for more than twenty years. He lives in Los Angeles with his wife and three daughters.

Additional Acknowledgements

Executive Publisher	Rich Rayburn
Associate Publisher	Kathy Krasenics
Project Management	Carol Kendall
Graphic Design	Emily Kattan, Mary Acree and Michele Cunningham-Scott
Production Coordinator	Kristy Randall, Jennifer Lenhart and Laura Greenwood
Editor	Elizabeth Gionta

THE PANACHE PORTFOLIO

The catalog of fine books in the areas of interior design and architecture and design continue to grow for Panache Partners, LLC. With more than 30 books published or in production, look for one or more of these keepsake books in a market near you.

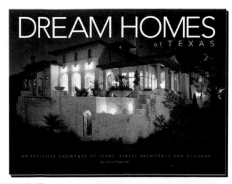

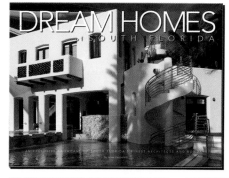

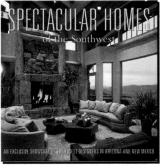

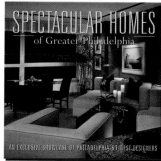

Spectacular Homes Series

Published in 2005
Spectacular Homes of Georgia
Spectacular Homes of South Florida
Spectacular Homes of Tennessee
Spectacular Homes of Texas

Published or Publishing in 2006
Spectacular Homes of California
Spectacular Homes of the Carolinas
Spectacular Homes of Chicago
Spectacular Homes of Colorado
Spectacular Homes of Florida
Spectacular Homes of Michigan
Spectacular Homes of the Pacific Northwest
Spectacular Homes of Greater Philadelphia
Spectacular Homes of the Southwest
Spectacular Homes of Washington DC

Other titles available from Panache Partners

Spectacular Hotels
Texans and Their Pets
Spectacular Restaurants of Texas

Dream Homes Series

Published in 2005
Dream Homes of Texas

Published or Publishing in 2006
Dream Homes of Colorado
Dream Homes of South Florida
Dream Homes of New Jersey
Dream Homes of New York
Dream Homes of Greater Philadelphia
Dream Homes of the Western Deserts

Order two or more copies today and we'll pay the shipping.

To order visit www.panache.com
or call 972.661.9884.

PANACHE
PARTNERS LLC

Creating Spectacular Publications for Discerning Readers

DESIGNERS INDEX